Frugal Feasts

101 Quick & Easy Single-Serving Meals from Around the World

■ ■ ■ ■ ■ ■ ■ ■ ■ ■ ■ ■ ■

Mary Spilsbury Ross

Doubleday
Toronto New York London
Sydney Auckland

Canadian Cataloguing in Publication Data

Ross, Mary Spilsbury
  Frugal feasts

ISBN 0-385-25529-2

1. Cookery for one. 2. Low budget cookery.
3. Quick and easy cookery. 4. Cookery, International
I. Title.

TX833. 5. R6   1996   641.5'61   C95-932389-9

Cover and text design by Avril Orloff
Printed and bound in the USA

Published in Canada by
Doubleday Canada Limited
105 Bond Street
Toronto, Ontario
M5B 1Y3

**Dedicated to all who are struggling with
rising prices and shrinking incomes.**

CONTENTS

PREFACE

The recipes in *Frugal Feasts* are based on the world's cheapest and most plentiful foodstuffs — rice, pasta, bread, beans and potatoes. Most of the recipes are well-loved classics, the traditional dishes often thought of as peasant food. The difference is that I have not only selected recipes with an eye to economy but have also adapted and simplified them to be cooked in twenty minutes or less with minimal preparation. The 101 meals, serving one generously or two modestly, have been carefully tested, timed, tasted and presented for a novice cook armed with only a pot, pan, wok and a few utensils. No microwaves, processors, blenders or beaters here — I'm talking simplicity!

Frugal Feasts started as an empty nest project that with the incredible enthusiasm of family and friends, quickly "souffléed." I would like to thank the following people for their support and help: Nora Clarke and Sally Wood, close and dear friends who cheerfully edited and corrected grammatical goofs and inconsistencies; Martin Scherzer, Allene Drake and Dale Wasson, who carefully scrutinized every recipe for clarity and simplicity; Moira Anderson of Village Books in Cadboro Bay; Sally Seyd Kimbell, owner of Mustards and Bistro à Vin in central London, a friend of more than thirty years who encouraged me to sample and appreciate exotic dishes throughout Europe and the Middle East; the late Dianne Winsby, whose book *I've Got to Have That Recipe!* inspired me to send my manuscript to be published; Michelle Peterson of Cadboro Bay Business Centre, who processed my messy notes over and over with unfailing humor and energy; Yole Barbon, whose skill in the *cucina* is an inspiration; my husband, Michael, who has encouraged me every step of the way and sampled the varied outcomes of reckless experiments; my children, Drew and Meg, who were the inspiration for the book and who urged me to complete it before they graduated; and lastly, my parents — my mother, Eleanore Spilsbury, for teaching me to be frugal, and my father, Richard Spilsbury, a mature student at "eightysomething" who is just now learning to cook and testing recipes from *Frugal Feasts*.

Eggs and Cheese

■ ■

Mexico

FRIED EGGS AND SALSA

(Huevos Rancheros)

This is a simple but superb Mexican favorite. Serve with corn or Refried Beans (page 74). If you like salsa "hot, hot, hot," add more jalapeño pepper!

1 tbsp (15 mL) vegetable oil

2 corn tortillas

2 eggs

½ cup (125 mL) Quick Homemade Salsa or
   commercial salsa

2 tbsp (25 mL) grated Cheddar or farmer's
   cheese

❶ Pour thin layer of oil in frying pan and lightly fry tortillas on both sides over medium heat. Remove from pan and keep warm.

❷ Reduce heat to low, add a few drops of oil to pan and fry eggs. Place eggs on top of tortillas.

❸ Cover eggs with salsa and grated cheese. Place under broiler for 1 minute to melt cheese and warm salsa.

QUICK HOMEMADE SALSA

Finely chop 1 tomato, ½ green pepper, ½ mild onion, and 1 clove garlic. Combine with ½ tsp (2 mL) minced jalapeño pepper, 1 tbsp (15 mL) each apple cider vinegar (or another mild vinegar), tomato paste and water. Stir well and season with ½ tsp (2 mL) ground cumin and ¼ tsp (1 mL) salt. Taste and add more cumin if necessary.

IT IS IMPORTANT TO REMEMBER THAT EGGS FRIED IN A

SHALLOW LAYER OF OIL OR BUTTER MUST COOK OVER A

LOW TEMPERATURE TO PREVENT THE BOTTOMS FROM

BURNING WHILE THE TOPS COOK. I USE CANOLA OIL

BECAUSE IT IS CHOLESTEROL-FREE, TASTELESS AND ONE

OF THE LEAST EXPENSIVE OILS.

■■■■■■■■■■■■■■■■■■■■■■■■■■■■

France

POACHED EGGS IN MASHED POTATO NEST

(Oeufs Pochés)

*This colorful combination tastes as good as it looks. Green
beans would be a perfect accompaniment.*

2 medium baking potatoes, peeled and diced
1 to 2 tbsp (15 to 25 mL) butter
1 tbsp (15 mL) milk (optional)
½ cup (125 mL) diced cooked ham
1 tsp (5 mL) white vinegar
2 eggs
**1 to 2 tbsp (15 to 25 mL) grated Swiss or
    Cheddar cheese**

❶ In saucepan, bring 2 to 3 cups (500 to 750 mL)
water to boil. Add potatoes, cover and cook for 8 to
10 minutes or until just tender when pierced with a
fork (the smaller the dice, the faster they will cook).
Drain well and shake saucepan briefly over medium
heat to dry potatoes. Remove from heat and mash
with a potato masher until lump-free. Add butter
and, if a little dry, milk. Beat well and stir in ham.

❷ Spoon potato and ham mixture onto a pie plate
and make a hollow in the center. Cover with a lid to
keep warm.

❸ Carefully break eggs into a bowl. In small
saucepan, bring 2 inches (5 cm) water and vinegar to
boil. Stir water clockwise and while water is swirling,

slip eggs in and turn heat off. Cover saucepan and allow eggs to cook undisturbed for about 3 minutes. When the whites are opaque and the yolks are covered with a thin layer of white, they are done. Remove eggs with a slotted spoon and pop them into potato nest. Sprinkle with grated cheese and place under broiler until piping hot.

ADDING A BIT OF VINEGAR TO THE POACHING WATER

HELPS KEEP THE EGG WHITE FROM SCATTERING. POACHED

EGGS ARE SOMETIMES DIPPED INTO COLD WATER AFTER

THEY ARE DONE TO HALT THE COOKING PROCESS. I ONLY

DO THIS IF I AM POACHING EGGS FOR A CROWD.

■■■■■■■■■■■■■■■■■■■■■■■■■■■■■

Germany
BACON VEGETABLE OMELET
(Bauernfrühstück)

Bauernfrühstück or "farmer's breakfast" is easy to make, filling and good at any time of the day. Serve flat like a pizza with multi-grain toast on the side.

1 large potato, peeled and thickly sliced
1 large carrot, scrubbed and thickly sliced
½ cup (125 mL) frozen green peas
2 slices bacon, chopped
¼ tsp (1 mL) marjoram
¼ tsp (1 mL) nutmeg
¼ tsp (1 mL) black pepper
1 or 2 tsp (5 or 10 mL) butter or vegetable oil
2 eggs, lightly beaten with a fork

❶ In saucepan, bring 1½ cups (375 mL) water to boil. Add potato and carrot slices, cover and boil for 8 to 10 minutes or until just tender when pierced with a fork. Add peas and cook for 1 minute until peas are thawed. Drain.

❷ In frying pan, fry bacon over medium-high heat for 2 to 3 minutes. Add drained vegetables, marjoram, nutmeg and pepper. With a spatula, lift and turn mixture until heated. Remove pan from heat, place bacon mixture on a plate and cover with a lid to keep warm.

❸ Return pan to heat and increase heat to high. Coat bottom of pan with butter or oil. Pour in beaten eggs, give pan a shake, spoon vegetables and bacon on top and spread out with back of spoon. Cover pan, remove from heat, and let stand for 1 minute until omelet has set completely.

SERVES ONE

Iran

VEGETABLE WALNUT OMELET
(Kuku ye Sabzi)

I first tasted this delicious green and crunchy egg dish in Teheran in 1964 during the city-wide celebration for the fifth birthday of the son of the Shah. It was served cold as a picnic dish, but I prefer to serve it hot with Basmati Rice (page 58) and yogurt.

2 eggs
1 cup (250 mL) finely chopped mixed leafy
  green vegetables (lettuce, spinach, parsley)
3 green onions, chopped
⅓ cup (75 mL) walnuts, chopped
¼ tsp (1 mL) salt
¼ tsp (1 mL) black pepper
1 tbsp (15 mL) butter

SERVES ONE

❶ In bowl, beat eggs until light and fluffy. Add chopped leafy vegetables, green onion, nuts, salt and pepper and mix well.

❷ In small frying pan, melt butter over medium-high heat and swirl to coat bottom of pan. Pour in egg mixture and smooth top with back of spoon. Cook for 1 minute or until bottom is set. Run a knife around edge to loosen and then invert omelet onto a plate.

❸ Return pan to heat, add a bit more butter if bottom of pan looks dry, and slide omelet back into pan to finish cooking on the other side. The eggs will set within about 30 seconds if the pan is hot enough. (An omelet that is cooked slowly loses its moistness.) Cut into wedges and serve on a warm plate.

■ ■

Japan

OMELET WITH GINGER CHICKEN
(Torimaki)

The sparkle of freshly grated ginger turns this omelet into something special. Try making Sushi Rice (page 66) and serve with a sliced cucumber salad.

½ cup (125 mL) shredded cooked chicken
2 tbsp (25 mL) soy sauce
1 tsp (5 mL) granulated sugar
1 ½-inch (5-cm) piece fresh ginger root, peeled
  and grated
2 eggs
1 tbsp (15 mL) water
1 tbsp (15 mL) vegetable oil (flavored with
  sesame oil if you have it)

❶ In small bowl, mix shredded chicken with 1 tbsp (15 mL) soy sauce, sugar and grated ginger.

❷ In another bowl, lightly beat eggs with 1 tbsp (15 mL) soy sauce and water.

❸ In small frying pan, heat oil over high heat and pour in egg mixture.Tilt pan and lift edge of omelet with tip of knife to let uncooked egg slide underneath. When top of omelet is still moist but not runny, spoon chicken mixture over one half and fold in two. A two-egg omelet will not take longer than 1 minute to set.

❹ Slide onto a warm plate and serve with extra soy sauce.

■ ■

Spain

SPANISH POTATO OMELET

(Tortilla a la Española)

A Spanish omelet is one of the most satisfying and quickly made supper dishes. I always serve it with warm tomato and green pepper chunks but if pushed for time, a dollop of tomato ketchup could be substituted.

4 tbsp (60 mL) olive oil (preferably Spanish)
1 large potato, scrubbed and very thinly sliced
1 medium onion, sliced
Salt and pepper to taste
2 eggs, beaten

❶ Place frying pan over medium-low heat and add oil. Layer potato and onion slices in pan and cook for about 8 minutes, lifting and turning with spatula, until tender when pierced with a fork but not crispy. Season with salt and pepper.

❷ Remove potato and onion from pan, increase heat to medium-high, and pour in beaten eggs. Immediately return potatoes and onions to pan, spreading evenly over eggs. Cook for 1 minute or until brown underneath.

❸ Invert plate over frying pan and flip omelet onto plate. Return pan to heat, add a drop of oil and slide omelet into pan to brown on other side. (If you hesitate to flip the omelet, simply brown the top under a preheated broiler.) Slide onto a warm plate and cut into wedges.

SERVES ONE

■ ■

China

EGGS AND BEAN SPROUTS

(Egg Foo Yong)

SERVES ONE

This is a fast and very good omelet with a slightly sweet sauce. Serve with rice and a tossed salad. For a different salad, try sliced bok choy or Chinese cabbage. This refreshing and crunchy cabbage is usually far more reasonably priced than imported, out-of-season head lettuce.

SAUCE

2 to 3 tbsp (25 to 45 mL) soy sauce
¼ cup (50 mL) cold water
½ tsp (2 mL) granulated sugar
½ tsp (2 mL) cornstarch

OMELET

2 eggs
1 tsp (5 mL) soy sauce
¼ tsp (1 mL) black pepper
1 tbsp (15 mL) vegetable oil (flavored with
    sesame oil if you have it)
1 small onion, finely chopped, or
3 green onions
2 stalks celery, sliced
¾ cup (175 mL) fresh bean sprouts
½ cup (125 mL) finely sliced cooked chicken or
    pork or diced tofu

❶ *Sauce:* In small saucepan, combine sauce ingredients. Stir and cook over medium heat until thickened. Keep warm over low heat while making omelet.

❷ *Omelet:* In small bowl, lightly beat eggs with soy sauce and pepper.

❸ Place frying pan over medium-high heat and add oil. Stir in green onion, celery and bean sprouts. Stir-fry for 1 minute or just until vegetables wilt. Add meat and continue to stir-fry for another 30 seconds. Remove from pan with slotted spoon.

❹ Pour egg mixture into same pan. Immediately spoon vegetables and meat on top of eggs, give one quick stir and cook for 1 minute. Remove from heat and flip with spatula like a pancake. Return to heat and cook the other side for 30 seconds or until eggs are set. Fold in half or serve flat. Slide onto a warm plate and pour sauce on top.

FRESH BEAN SPROUTS MUST BE USED FOR THIS RECIPE. FOR A CONTINUAL SUPPLY, CONSIDER SPROUTING YOUR OWN. MUNG BEANS SPROUT IN A MATTER OF DAYS IN A DARK, COOL CUPBOARD. HEALTH FOOD STORES USUALLY SELL AN INEXPENSIVE PLASTIC "SPROUTER" ALONG WITH MUNG BEANS AND SIMPLE INSTRUCTIONS.

India

GOVERNMENT HOUSE CURRIED EGGS

(Anda Kari)

This Anglo-Indian recipe from a faded old book of my mother's, dated 1915, is still a winner eighty years later. Pour eggs and sauce over hot cooked rice and dig in.

1 tbsp (15 mL) butter
1 onion, sliced
1 tbsp (15 mL) curry powder
1 tsp (5 mL) all-purpose flour
1 apple, chopped
1 clove garlic, crushed
1 tbsp (15 mL) chutney or lemon juice
½ to 1 cup (125 to 250 mL) chicken or vegetable
   stock or water
2 hard-cooked eggs

❶ In frying pan, melt butter over medium heat. Add sliced onion, curry powder and flour. Stir and cook for 2 to 3 minutes or until onion is golden.

❷ Add apple, garlic, chutney and ½ cup (125 mL) stock, stir well and simmer over medium heat for 5 minutes or until thickened and bubbling. If it gets too thick, add ¼ cup (75 mL) liquid.

❸ Cut eggs in half and add to curry sauce. Cover pan and simmer for another minute to heat eggs.

■ ■

Czech Republic

CRISPY CHEESE CUTLETS

(Syř Smažený)

This old-fashioned recipe has reappeared in trendy pubs all over the country. Serve with buttered noodles and apple, pear or watermelon wedges.

2 or 3 thick slices Swiss or mild white cheese
1 to 2 tbsp (15 to 25 mL) all-purpose flour
1 egg, beaten
½ to ¾ cup (125 to 175 mL) dry bread crumbs
2 to 3 tbsp (25 to 45 mL) vegetable oil

❶ Dip cheese slices in flour, then in beaten egg and finally in bread crumbs. Let stand a moment before redipping in egg and crumbs until cheese is completely covered in a thick coating.

❷ In frying pan, heat oil over medium heat. Don't overheat oil or coating will burn before cheese is melted. Cook breaded cheese for 2 minutes or until golden.

❸ With a spatula, carefully turn cheese and cook for another 2 minutes until the outside is crisp and the inside melted.

SERVES ONE

TO PREVENT CHEESE FROM DRYING OUT, TRY WRAPPING IT IN A VINEGAR-SOAKED CLOTH. ODD BITS AND PIECES OF DRIED-OUT CHEDDAR AND OTHER FIRM CHEESES CAN BE GRATED, PUT IN A RECYCLED PLASTIC CONTAINER AND STORED IN THE FREEZER TO BE SPRINKLED ON SALADS, NACHOS, PASTA, BEANS OR BAKED POTATOES.

■■■■■■■■■■■■■■■■■■■■■■■■■■■■■■

Switzerland

SWISS TOAST WITH HAM AND CHEESE

(Croque-Monsieur)

This is a classic recipe that is adored all over Europe. I always serve it with pickled beets and whatever leafy green is in season.

2 slices Swiss cheese
1 medium-thick slice cooked ham
1 tsp (5 mL) Dijon mustard (optional)
2 thick slices French bread, buttered
2 eggs
¼ tsp (1 mL) nutmeg
¼ tsp (1 mL) black pepper
1 to 2 tbsp (15 to 25 mL) butter or vegetable oil

❶ Arrange a slice of cheese, the ham, the second slice of cheese and a layer of Dijon mustard, if using, between slices of buttered bread and press firmly together.

❷ In shallow dish, beat eggs with nutmeg and pepper. Dip sandwich into egg mixture and soak both sides until egg has been completely absorbed.

❸ Place frying pan over medium-low heat and add butter or oil or a mixture of both. Cook sandwich for 2 to 3 minutes. Turn and cook the other side for 2 minutes or until bread is golden and cheese is melted.

SERVES ONE

■ ■

England
CHEESE AND APPLE TOAST

These toasted sandwiches, also known as Poor Knights, are the perfect light supper when supplies are running low. Serve with a leafy green salad.

SERVES ONE

1 to 2 tbsp (15 to 25 mL) butter
1 apple, finely diced
½ tsp (2 mL) lemon juice
¼ tsp (1 mL) nutmeg
¼ tsp(1 mL) black pepper
¼ tsp (1 mL) salt
2 thick slices unbuttered toast
½ cup (125 mL) grated Cheddar cheese

❶ In frying pan, melt butter over medium-low heat. Add apple and lemon juice, stir and cook for 2 minutes or until apple begins to soften. Season with nutmeg, pepper and salt.

❷ Place toast on baking sheet and spoon an equal amount of apple mixture onto each slice. Top with grated cheese and place under preheated broiler until cheese is melted and bubbling. Watch carefully; it will be ready in less than a minute. Slide onto a warm plate.

APPLES NEED TO BE KEPT COOL AND DRY. THEY BREATHE DURING STORAGE, SO WRAP IN NEWSPRINT AND PUT IN BOXES AWAY FROM OTHER VEGETABLES. APPLES THAT STORE WELL INCLUDE: WINESAP, JONATHAN, McINTOSH AND DELICIOUS.

■■■■■■■■■■■■■■■■■■■■■■■■■■■■■■■

Mexico

CHEESE TORTILLAS WITH SALSA

(Quesadillas)

This Mexican-style toasted cheese sandwich is delicious garnished with hot salsa and cool sour cream. For a more substantial meal, serve with Refried Beans (page 74) and corn.

½ to ¾ cup (125 to 175 mL) grated Monterey Jack or brick cheese

1 tomato, chopped

3 green onions, chopped

1 clove garlic, minced

¼ tsp (1 mL) salt

1 or 2 drops hot Tabasco sauce, or

Pinch dried chili peppers

½ tsp (2 mL) ground coriander

2 soft flour tortillas (7½ inches/19 cm in diameter)

2 to 3 tbsp (25 to 45 mL) Quick Homemade Salsa (page 8) or commercial salsa

1 dollop sour cream (optional)

❶ In small bowl, mix together cheese, tomato, green onion, garlic, salt, Tabasco sauce and coriander. Spread half of cheese mixture on half of one tortilla, making sure it is evenly distributed. Fold over and press down on ingredients with palm of your hand to form a half moon. Repeat with second tortilla and remaining cheese mixture.

❷ Heat large frying pan over medium heat until very hot. Using a spatula, place folded tortilla in pan. Cook, pressing down with spatula, until cheese melts and tortilla is slightly brown, 3 to 4 minutes on each side. Repeat with second tortilla.

❸ To serve, cut quesadillas in half and garnish with salsa and a dollop of sour cream, if using.

A SPANISH TORTILLA AND A MEXICAN TORTILLA ARE TWO ENTIRELY DIFFERENT FOODS. THE FORMER IS AN OMELET, USUALLY A POTATO ONE, AND THE LATTER IS A FLAT, PANCAKE-LIKE BREAD MADE OF CORNMEAL OR WHEAT FLOUR.

■■■■■■■■■■■■■■■■■■■■■■■■■■■■■■

Poland

COTTAGE CHEESE PIEROGI
(Pierogi Leniwe)

Called "lazy" pierogi in Polish, these light and fluffy puffs are easy and delightfully different.

2 eggs, lightly beaten
1 cup (250 mL) cottage cheese
¾ cup (175 mL) all-purpose flour
¼ tsp (1 mL) salt
¼ tsp (1 mL) black pepper
1 tbsp (15 mL) butter
¼ cup (50 mL) dry bread crumbs
¼ cup (50 mL) grated Cheddar or Parmesan cheese
3 green onions, chopped

❶ In bowl, mix together lightly beaten eggs, cottage cheese, flour, salt and pepper until mixture resembles soft dough.

❷ On floured counter, pat or roll mixture into a rectangle about ½ inch (1 cm) thick. Cut into 1 x 1-inch (2.5 x 2.5-cm) squares.

❸ Bring large pot of water to boil. Add squares, reduce heat to low and simmer for 5 minutes or until they float to top. Drain and place in a bowl. Toss with butter and sprinkle with bread crumbs, cheese and green onion.

SERVES ONE

SOUPS

■■■■■■■■■■■■■■■■■■■■■■■■■■■■■■■■

Canada
BASIC MEAT STOCK
(Fond ordinaire)

MAKES APPROXIMATELY 10 CUPS (2.5 L)

Making soup from scratch in 20 minutes for a single meal is not very practical, so I have included only five soup recipes in this chapter. However, it is great to have on hand a meat stock to add flavor to canned soups, sauces and risottos.

4 lb (1.8 kg) mixed bones and meat
(beef, chicken, turkey or a combination)
2 medium onions, unpeeled
2 carrots, scrubbed but not peeled
½ cup (125 mL) celery tops
1 tsp (5 mL) each crushed bay leaves and thyme
2 tsp (10 mL) salt

❶ Put bones and meat in large pot. Cover with cold water and bring to boil. If any scum rises to surface, skim off with a slotted spoon.

❷ Add onions (skins give the stock a dark color), carrots, celery tops and seasoning. Reduce heat, cover and simmer for about 4 hours.

❸ Strain stock and cool. The fat will rise to the surface and harden. Lift it off and discard. Use stock immediately or freeze in jam jars (leave 1 inch/2.5 cm head space for expansion as it freezes). For smaller amounts, freeze in ice cube trays and store cubes in plastic freezer bags. Approximately 9 cubes equal 1 cup (250 mL).

IF STOCK IS STORED IN THE REFRIGERATOR, IT MUST BE

REBOILED EVERY DAY TO KEEP IT FROM GOING SOUR.

■ ■

Ireland
POTATO, ONION AND BACON SOUP

I love the comfort of Irish potato soup and warm crusty rolls, especially on a dreary winter's night. It makes me think of great-great-grandfather Haggarty of County Cork.

1 tbsp (15 mL) butter or vegetable oil
1 large onion, chopped
2 or 3 slices bacon, chopped
1 tbsp (15 mL) all-purpose flour
1 cup (250 mL) vegetable or chicken stock or water
1 large baking potato, peeled and diced
¼ tsp (1 mL) each nutmeg and salt
½ tsp (2 mL) black pepper
¼ cup (50 mL) light cream or milk
1 tsp (5 mL) butter (optional

❶ In large saucepan, cook butter, onion and bacon over medium-low heat for 4 to 5 minutes or until onion is transparent and bacon has rendered its fat. Sprinkle in flour and stir well.

❷ Add stock, potato, nutmeg, salt and ¼ tsp (1 mL) pepper. Bring to boil, reduce heat and simmer until potato cubes are tender when pierced with a fork, approximately 10 minutes. Add extra stock if too dry.

❸ Stir in cream and heat (do not boil). Pour into soup bowl, swirl in butter, if using, and sprinkle with ¼ tsp (1 mL) pepper.

SERVES ONE

■■■■■■■■■■■■■■■■■■■■■■■■■■■■■■■

Algeria
SPICED LENTIL SOUP
(Chorba 'dess)

Rich in flavor but not in cost, this spicy soup is truly a meal in itself. Serve with pita bread or toast brushed with olive oil.

½ cup (125 mL) red lentils
3 tbsp (45 mL) olive or vegetable oil
1 medium onion, chopped
1 clove garlic, minced
¼ tsp (1 mL) each ground coriander, ground
  cumin, cinnamon, turmeric, black pepper
  and cayenne pepper
1 large carrot, scrubbed or peeled and grated
1 large potato, peeled and grated
2 cups (500 mL) vegetable stock, tomato juice
  or water
¼ tsp (1 mL) salt

❶ Pour boiling water over lentils and let them soften while preparing vegetables. Drain before using.

❷ In saucepan, warm oil over medium heat. Add onion and cook for 1 to 2 minutes or until onion is transparent. Stir in garlic, spices, drained lentils, carrot, potato and stock. Cover and simmer over low heat until vegetables are cooked, about 15 minutes. Stir occasionally and add a little more stock if soup is too thick.

❸ Add salt, taste and adjust seasoning.

DRIED LENTILS, BLACK-EYED PEAS AND SPLIT PEAS ARE THE

ONLY LEGUMES THAT DO NOT REQUIRE OVERNIGHT SOAKING.

■■■■■■■■■■■■■■■■■■■■■■■■■■■■■■

United States
BOSTON CLAM CHOWDER

A bowl of steaming hot, old-fashioned clam chowder has been a favorite maritime supper for decades. Serve with whole wheat toast or warm crusty rolls.

2 or 3 slices bacon, diced
1 medium onion, chopped
1 large baking potato, peeled and diced
½ can (10 oz/284 g) baby clams, undrained
½ cup (125 mL) water
1 cup (250 mL) milk
¼ tsp (1 mL) each salt and pepper, or to taste
1 tbsp (15 mL) butter

❶ In saucepan, fry bacon over medium heat for 2 minutes or until lightly browned. Add onion and cook for about 1 minute or until transparent. Stir in potato, clam liquid (approximately ½ cup/125 mL) and ½ cup (125 mL) water. Reduce heat to low, cover and simmer for 8 to 10 minutes or until potatoes are tender when pierced with a fork.

❷ Add clams (approximately ½ cup/125 mL), milk, salt and pepper and cook just until soup is piping hot. Do not allow soup to boil after milk has been added.

❸ Pour into warm soup bowl, swirl in butter and serve immediately.

A 10-oz (284-g) can of clams is expensive for the

budget cook unless it makes two meals. Consider

Boston Clam Chowder one night and Pasta with

Clam and Tomato Sauce (page 148) the following.

SERVES ONE

■ ■

St. Lucia

CARIBBEAN PUMPKIN SOUP

(Le Potage au Potiron)

Allspice and hot sauce, two flavors essential to West Indian cooking, combine to turn the lowly pumpkin into an unusual, colorful and delicious soup that is adored throughout the Caribbean Islands. Serve with a mixed green salad sprinkled with peanuts and croutons.

2 tbsp (25 mL) butter
1 medium onion, chopped
2 cups (500 mL) pumpkin or winter squash,
**   peeled and cubed**
2 cups (500 mL) vegetable or chicken stock
½ tsp (2 mL) granulated sugar
¼ tsp (1 mL) salt
½ tsp (2 mL) allspice or nutmeg
2 or 3 drops Tabasco sauce or cayenne pepper
4 tbsp (60 mL) cream or stock (optional)
4 tbsp (60 mL) slivered cooked ham (optional)

❶ In saucepan, melt butter over medium heat. Add onion and cook for 2 to 3 minutes or until transparent. Add pumpkin, stock, sugar and salt, mix well and cook gently over medium-low heat for 10 minutes or until pumpkin is very tender.

❷ Mash pumpkin with a potato masher and season with allspice and Tabasco sauce. (Whirl in a blender if you have one, but it is not essential.)

SERVES TWO

❸ Thin with a little cream, if necessary. Pour into warm soup bowl and garnish with ham slivers, if using.

OF ALL WINTER VEGETABLES, SQUASHES SUCH AS ACORN, BUTTERNUT, HUBBARD OR PUMPKIN ARE A TERRIFIC BUY FOR BUDGET SHOPPERS. KEEP WHOLE SQUASH IN A COOL, DRY AREA. CUT SQUASH SHOULD BE WRAPPED IN A PLASTIC BAG AND REFRIGERATED.

■■■■■■■■■■■■■■■■■■■■■■■■■■■■■■

Turkey
CHICKEN NOODLE SOUP
(Sehriyeli Çorbasi)

SERVES ONE

Fresh lemon juice is an important ingredient in Turkish dishes. In this very quick and simple chicken noodle soup, it adds a refreshing and subtle tang. Serve with a green salad or Chick Pea Dip with Vegetables (page 34).

4 oz (125 mL) boneless, skinless chicken
2 cups (500 mL) chicken stock (salt free)
1 tsp (5 mL) butter
¼ tsp (1 mL) each salt and pepper
½ cup (60 g) broken vermicelli
1 egg yolk beaten with a fork
½ lemon

❶ Cut chicken into finger sized slices.

❷ In saucepan, combine chicken, stock, butter, salt and pepper over high heat and bring to a boil. Stir well, cover with a lid and turn heat down to medium low. Simmer for 10 minutes.

❸ Add vermicelli, stir to separate the strands and simmer uncovered for an additional 10 minutes.

❹ In a large soup bowl, beat egg yolk with a fork. Add lemon juice beating constantly. Pour hot soup gradually into the bowl, stirring vigorously. (The hot soup will cook the egg instantly). Serve immediately.

SALADS

■■■■■■■■■■■■■■■■■■■■■■■■■■■■■■

Lebanon
CHICK PEA DIP WITH VEGETABLES
(Hummus bi Tahini)

SERVES ONE

I first tasted this delicious, creamy bean puree many years ago in Beirut. My Lebanese hosts served it with an amazing assortment of raw vegetables and pita bread for dipping. In many parts of the eastern Mediterranean it is eaten as a breakfast dish. Serve with raw vegetables and warm flatbread.

1 cup (250 mL) cooked chick peas
⅓ cup (75 mL) water
4 tbsp (60 mL) olive oil
Juice of 1 lemon
2 cloves garlic, crushed
½ tsp (2 mL) each salt and ground cumin
¼ tsp (1 mL) black pepper
2 tbsp (25 mL) sesame paste (tahini)
½ tsp (2 mL) paprika
Green pepper strips, romaine lettuce leaves,
 pickles, zucchini sticks, cucumber spears
 and flatbread

❶ In saucepan, bring chick peas and water to boil. Cover and cook over medium-low heat for 5 minutes to soften. Mash with a potato masher, making as smooth a puree as possible. If you have a food processor, you do not have to cook the beans — simply puree with ⅓ cup (75 mL) warm water.

❷ Beat in 3 tbsp (45 mL) olive oil, lemon juice, garlic, salt, cumin, pepper and sesame paste.

❸ Spread warm hummus on plate. Drizzle with 1 tbsp (15 mL) olive oil and sprinkle with paprika.

■■■■■■■■■■■■■■■■■■■■■■■■■■■■■■■

Russia

POTATO, SAUSAGE AND CHICKEN SALAD

(Salat Oliviye)

This potato salad recipe, from a friend who was born on the Russian-Iranian border, is the most delicious I have ever eaten.

3 medium potatoes, peeled and diced
½ cup (125 g) diced cooked chicken
6 to 8 slices Kielbasa sausage
2 or 3 tbsp (25 or 45 mL) chopped dill pickles
¼ cup (50 mL) green peas, thawed if frozen
1 large carrot, peeled and grated
¼ tsp (1 mL) salt
Pinch black pepper
¼ cup (50 mL) mayonnaise
1 or 2 tbsp (15 or 25 mL) pickle juice
Mixed leafy greens
1 hard-cooked egg, peeled and sliced (optional)

❶ In medium saucepan, drop diced potatoes into 4 cups (1 L) cold water. Cover and bring to boil. Cook for 8 to 10 minutes or until tender when pierced with a fork. Drain potatoes, place in mixing bowl and cool to room temperature.

❷ Add chicken, sausage, pickles, peas, carrot, salt and pepper and thoroughly mix.

❸ Stir in mayonnaise and pickle juice. Arrange salad over a bed of mixed leafy greens and garnish with sliced egg, if using.

SERVES ONE OR TWO

■ ■

Mexico

HOT CHICKEN CAESAR

(Ensalada con Pollo y Anchoa)

Serve this bistro-style grilled chicken piled on top of a classic Caesar salad for a light supper.

1 chicken breast, boned with skin removed
1 tbsp (15 mL) vegetable oil
Pinch black pepper
¼ tsp (1 mL) tarragon (or favorite herb)
6 or 8 romaine lettuce leaves

....

CAESAR DRESSING

1 egg
2 tbsp (25 mL) lemon juice
1 or 2 cloves garlic, minced
¼ tsp (1 mL) salt
Pinch pepper
4 tbsp (60 mL) olive oil (or a mixture of
   vegetable oil flavored with olive oil)
1 tbsp (15 mL) Parmesan cheese
1 or 2 anchovy fillets, chopped (optional)
Toasted croutons (optional)

❶ Preheat broiler. Brush chicken with oil and sprinkle with pepper and tarragon. Place on broiling pan and grill, turning often, for 8 to 10 minutes or until meat is tender and no longer pink inside.

SERVES ONE

❷ Trim, wash and dry lettuce. Tear into bite-sized pieces and place in bowl.

❸ *Caesar Dressing:* Coddle egg by gently lowering it into pot of boiling water. Turn off heat and allow to cook for approximately 40 seconds. Remove egg and plunge it into cold water to prevent further cooking. In medium bowl, whisk together egg, lemon juice, garlic, salt, pepper and oil.

❹ Pour dressing over lettuce. Sprinkle with Parmesan cheese and anchovies, if using, and toss. Top with hot sliced chicken breast and garnish with toasted croutons if desired.

The original recipe from Tijuana did not include anchovies, but I think their saltiness adds an exciting tang. Leftover anchovies when finely chopped are a delicious addition to pizza and to tomato sauce for pasta. When mixed with soy sauce, they make a substitute for Thai fish sauce.

SERVES ONE

Malaysia

VEGETABLE SALAD WITH PEANUT DRESSING

(Gado Gado)

In Malaysia and Indonesia, Gado Gado is a favorite salad of tourists and locals alike. Try it. You will love the combination of tender, crisp vegetables bathed in a pungent peanut dressing.

1 large carrot, peeled and cut into sticks
6 green beans, cut into bite-sized pieces
½ cup (125 mL) fresh bean sprouts
1 large potato, boiled and sliced (use leftovers)
3 or 4 slices cucumber
2 hard-cooked eggs, peeled and halved
1 cup (250 mL) shredded lettuce leaves

PEANUT DRESSING

1 tbsp (15 mL) vegetable oil
1 small onion, finely chopped
1 clove garlic, minced
1 tsp (5 mL) minced hot chili pepper
¼ tsp (1 mL) each salt and granulated sugar
1 tbsp (15 mL) soy sauce
¼ cup (50 mL) coconut milk or water
   (see note below)
3 tbsp (45 mL) peanut butter

❶ In small saucepan, bring about 2 cups (500 mL) water to boil and put in carrot sticks. Cover and cook for 1 minute. Uncover, add green beans and cook for another minute. Toss in bean sprouts, give a quick stir, drain immediately and rinse under cold water to prevent further cooking.

❷ On a plate, arrange cold sliced potato, carrot, green beans, bean sprouts, cucumber and halved eggs over bed of shredded lettuce.

❸ *Peanut Dressing:* Place small frying pan over medium heat and pour in oil. Add onion, garlic, chili pepper, salt and sugar and stir-fry for 30 seconds until fragrant. Add soy sauce, coconut milk and peanut butter and reduce heat to low. Simmer, stirring constantly, until dressing is thickened and heated through. Serve immediately as a dipping sauce or spooned over vegetables.

Coconut milk or cream can be purchased as an instant powder to be mixed with water, or you can make your own. See page 62 for instructions using desiccated coconut.

■ ■

Greece

PASTA SALAD WITH FETA AND OLIVES

(Salátes mè Feta)

This is my daughter's favorite light supper. Make a large bowl; it keeps well and the flavors meld overnight in the fridge. Serve with warm pita bread or toast.

1 lb (500 g) dried rotini or macaroni
1 medium onion, finely chopped
1 green pepper, chopped
1 or 2 tomatoes, chopped
1 cup (250 mL) sliced cucumber, halved
1 cup (250 mL feta cheese, crumbled
1 cup (250 mL) sliced black olives, drained

....

DRESSING

4 tbsp (60 mL) olive oil
4 tbsp (60 mL) apple cider vinegar
1 tsp (5 mL) Dijon mustard
½ tsp (2 mL) each basil and oregano
¼ tsp (1 mL) salt
Pinch black pepper

❶ In large pot of boiling, salted water, cook rotini for 8 to 10 minutes. Drain and rinse with cold water. Toss with vegetables, cheese and olives.

❷ *Dressing:* In small bowl, mix all ingredients.

❸ Pour dressing over pasta and vegetables and toss. Serve at room temperature.

SERVES THREE OR FOUR

POTATOES

■■■■■■■■■■■■■■■■■■■■■■■■■■■■■

Germany

MASHED POTATOES AND APPLES

(Himmel und Erde)

This Old World favorite, Heaven and Earth, is a slightly sweet and sour potato dish that is the perfect accompaniment for pork chops, baked ham or sausages.

SERVES ONE

¼ cup (50 mL) water
1 tbsp (15 mL) cider vinegar
¼ tsp (1 mL) salt
½ tsp (2 mL) granulated sugar
2 medium apples, peeled and cubed
2 medium potatoes, peeled and cubed
1 tbsp (15 mL) butter
¼ tsp (1 mL) marjoram
¼ tsp (1 mL) black pepper

❶ In saucepan, combine water, vinegar, salt and sugar. Add cubed apples and potatoes. Bring to boil, cover and reduce heat to simmer. Cook for 10 minutes or until potatoes are tender when pierced with a fork. If apples are not very juicy, you may need to add more water to keep potato mixture from drying out.

❷ Remove from heat and mash potatoes and apples with a potato masher until smooth. Stir in butter, marjoram and pepper.

WHEN SELECTING POTATOES, LOOK FOR SMOOTH SKINS THAT ARE FREE FROM BLEMISHES AND ANY SIGN OF SPOTTING. NEVER BUY GREENISH-LOOKING POTATOES; THEY CAN BE TOXIC.

France

POTATOES WITH CHEESE AND CREAM

(Pommes de Terre Savoyards)

This wonderful creamy potato dish is so rich that it needs only a crisp, fresh salad to complete the meal.

SERVES TWO

4 medium new waxy potatoes, scrubbed
2 cloves garlic
2 tbsp (25 mL) vegetable oil
3 tbsp (45 mL) butter
½ cup (125 mL) shredded Gruyère cheese
½ tsp (2 mL) nutmeg
¼ tsp (1 mL) each salt and pepper
4 tbsp (60 mL) cream

❶ Slice potatoes thinly and put in pot with 3 cups (750 mL) salted water. Bring to boil and cook for 3 minutes. Drain.

❷ Rub garlic over bottom of cast-iron pan and add oil. Layer half the potatoes in pan, dot with butter and sprinkle on half the cheese. Sprinkle with half the nutmeg, salt and pepper. Layer remaining potatoes, cheese and seasoning. Cover with lid or heavy, heat-proof plate and cook over medium heat for 10 minutes. Add cream, cover again and reduce heat to low. Simmer for another 10 minutes or until potatoes are tender when pierced with a fork.

❸ Uncover and place under broiler for 1 minute or until top is golden brown. Invert onto a warm plate and cut into wedges like a pie.

■ ■

Mexico
POTATO MOZZARELLA PIE
(Patatas con Queso)

If you like nachos, you'll love this cheesy potato pie. Serve with Quick Homemade Salsa (page 8) and sour cream.

SERVES ONE

2 medium potatoes, peeled and cubed
2 tbsp (25 mL) olive oil
¼ tsp (1 mL) salt
Pinch black pepper
½ cup (125 mL) Refried Beans (page 74) or
  cooked pinto beans
¼ to ½ cup (50 to 125 mL) grated mozzarella
1 small green chili pepper, chopped
2 or 3 green onions, chopped

❶ Boil potato cubes in 2 cups (500 mL) salted water for 6 to 8 minutes or until not quite done. Drain and place in oiled oven-proof pan. Add salt and pepper.

❷ Top potatoes with dollops of refried beans. Do not try to smooth them out. Cover with cheese, chili pepper and green onion.

❸ Bake for 10 minutes in 400° F (200° C) oven until cheese melts and potatoes are tender when pierced.

FRESH MOZZARELLA HAS A SPONGY TEXTURE AND A MILD

TASTE. AS THIS CHEESE AGES, IT BECOMES DRIER AND MORE

ELASTIC. AGED MOZZARELLA IS ONE OF THE CHEAPER

CHEESES, AND A GOOD SOURCE OF PROTEIN FOR THE

BUDGET SHOPPER.

■ ■

Russia
POTATO PANCAKES
(Dranniki)

These pancakes are simply marvelous with crisp bacon, warm applesauce, or hot sliced apples and a dollop of sour cream.

2 medium baking or winter potatoes, peeled
1 small onion, grated
1 egg, beaten with a fork
¼ cup (50 mL) all-purpose flour
¼ tsp (1 mL) salt
Pinch black pepper
2 tbsp (25 mL) vegetable oil

❶ Grate potatoes and onion onto tea towel, squeeze dry and place in a bowl. Add beaten egg, flour, salt and pepper, and stir very well.

❷ Place frying pan over medium heat and add 1 tsp (5 mL) oil. Drop 1 heaping serving spoon of potato mixture into hot oil. Flatten as much as possible or pancake will not cook evenly. Fry until golden and crisp on the outside and tender inside.

❸ Place pancake on a plate and keep warm in oven. Add another drop or two of oil to frying pan and continue making pancakes until batter is used up.

ALWAYS HEAT A FRYING PAN OR WOK BEFORE ADDING
ANY OIL. THIS HELPS KEEP FOOD FROM STICKING.

SERVES ONE

■ ■

India

POTATO CURRY WITH PEANUTS

(Sabzi Ka Kari)

SERVES ONE

A pungent and aromatic dish using the humble potato. With most curry dinners I like to serve fried papadums or Indian flat bread, which is available in supermarkets and bulk food shops. They are deliciously addictive — a bit like giant potato chips.

1 large potato, peeled and diced
1 large carrot, scrubbed and diced
1 tbsp (15 mL) vegetable oil
1 large onion, chopped
1 or 2 cloves garlic, crushed
1 tsp (5 mL) (or more) curry powder
½ tsp (2 mL) ground cumin
1 tbsp (15 mL) tomato paste or ketchup
½ lemon, juice and grated rind (yellow
   skin only)
¼ tsp (1 mL) salt
¼ cup (50 mL) peanuts

❶ Boil potato and carrot in about 2 cups (500 mL) water for 3 to 4 minutes. Drain and reserve liquid.

❷ Place frying pan over medium heat and pour in oil. Add onion and cook for 1 or 2 minutes or until transparent. Add garlic, curry powder and cumin. Stir well and continue cooking for another minute.

❸ Add tomato paste thinned with about 1 cup (250 mL) reserved vegetable water. Use just enough water to make a thick gravy. Stir until well blended. Add potato, carrot, lemon juice and rind, and salt. Cover pan, reduce heat to low and simmer until vegetables are tender and heated through. Sprinkle with peanuts and serve with yogurt, if desired.

AFTER SOYBEANS, PEANUTS PACK THE MOST PROTEIN

VALUE OF ALL NON-MEAT FOODS AND CONTAIN MOSTLY

UNSATURATED FAT.

■■■■■■■■■■■■■■■■■■■■■■■■■■■■■■■

England

PERFECT MASHED POTATOES

Every budget cook needs to know how to make perfect mashed potatoes to serve with the humble "banger" whether it be a pork, beef or vegetarian sausage. Onion gravy is an excellent sauce to ladle over the top.

2 large baking potatoes, peeled and quartered
1 egg
Salt and pepper to taste

SWEET ONION GRAVY

1 tbsp (15 mL) butter or vegetable oil
1 large onion, sliced
1 tbsp (15 mL) all-purpose flour
½ cup (125 mL) reserved potato water or stock
¼ cup (50 mL) red wine, beer or unsweetened
   fruit juice
1 tsp (5 mL) Dijon mustard
1 tsp (5 mL) granulated sugar (less if using
   fruit juice)
Dash Worcestershire sauce
Salt and pepper to taste

❶ Place potatoes in saucepan with enough salted water to cover. Bring to boil, cover, reduce heat to medium-low and simmer for 15 to 20 minutes or until potatoes are tender but still firm.

❷ Drain well, reserving potato water for gravy. Return pan briefly to stove; shake to dry potatoes.

Remove from heat, mash with a potato masher until fluffy, then add egg. Beat with spoon until smooth. Season with salt and pepper.

❸ *Sweet Onion Gravy:* In frying pan, melt butter over medium-low heat and cook onion for 3 to 4 minutes or until transparent. Stir in flour and mix well. Add potato water and wine and continue stirring. Bring to boil. Season with mustard, sugar, Worcestershire sauce, salt and pepper, and let it bubble for 2 to 3 minutes until thickened slightly.

WORCESTERSHIRE SAUCE IS A USEFUL SEASONING.

BECAUSE IT IS CONCENTRATED, A LITTLE GOES A LONG

WAY. USE IT TO PERK UP GRAVIES, MARINADES AND

SOUPS.

United States
PARMESAN POTATO WEDGES
(Oven Fries)

SERVES ONE

My family adores these crispy "oven fries" and insists they be included in this cookbook. They are perfect with fried eggs and complement grilled burgers or baked fish.

Vegetable oil
1 large baking potato, scrubbed but not peeled
¼ cup (50 mL) dry bread crumbs
2 tbsp (25 mL) grated Parmesan cheese
¼ tsp (1 mL) each salt, pepper and garlic
**   powder**
½ tsp (2 mL) paprika

❶ Coat bottom of pie plate with vegetable oil. Cut potato lengthwise into 6 or 8 equal-sized wedges and pat dry. Roll in oil in pie plate.

❷ Shake together bread crumbs, Parmesan cheese and seasoning in plastic or paper bag. Add potato wedges and shake to coat.

❸ Place wedges skin side down on oiled pie plate and bake in preheated 450° F (230° C) oven for 20 to 25 minutes. Drain on paper towel.

BAKING POTATOES KEEP WELL IF STORED IN A DARK, DRY PLACE WITH GOOD VENTILATION. IF SPACE IS LIMITED, CONSIDER A KITCHEN DRAWER WITH A RACK FOR AIR MOVEMENT. REMOVE FROM PLASTIC BAG AND PLACE IN A SINGLE LAYER.

■ ■

Hungary
POOR MAN'S GOULASH
(Paprikás Krumpli)

This is a superb, creamy potato dish that is simple to make and uses only one pan. I like to serve it with a crunchy celery and walnut salad for a contrast in texture.

2 or 3 tbsp (25 or 45 mL) vegetable oil
1 medium onion, roughly chopped
2 tsp paprika (10 mL) (see note below)
1 large potato, peeled and diced
½ green pepper, sliced
Pinch each salt and pepper
¼ cup (50 mL) water
2 or 3 slices cooked Hungarian sausage (optional)
2 or 3 tbsp (25 or 45 mL) sour cream

❶ Place frying pan over medium heat and add oil. Add onion and cook for 3 to 4 minutes or until transparent. Stir in paprika and add potato, green pepper, salt, pepper and water. Bring to boil.

❷ Reduce heat to simmer, cover and cook for 8 to 10 minutes or until potatoes are tender when pierced.

❸ Uncover and stir gently, ensuring that potato cubes are not crushed. Add sliced sausage and sour cream and heat through. Spoon onto a warm plate.

SERVES ONE

PAPRIKA IS MADE FROM DRIED RED PEPPERS. THE FLAVOR VARIES FROM MILD TO HOT. THE WORLD'S BEST PAPRIKA COMES FROM SZEGED, HUNGARY. TO KEEP PAPRIKA FRESH, STORE IN THE FREEZER.

■ ■

Italy

MASHED POTATO PIZZA

(Torta di Patate)

This is a versatile recipe that uses up odd bits and pieces in the fridge. Serve with a green salad sprinkled with chick peas.

2 large baking potatoes, peeled and cubed
¼ tsp (1 mL) salt
Pinch black pepper
1 tbsp (15 mL) olive oil
1 or 2 tomatoes, sliced
¼ to ½ cup (125 mL) shredded mozzarella
Optional pizza toppings: sliced olives, chopped
**   green pepper, anchovies, sliced smoked**
**   sausage, chopped green onions, minced garlic**
½ tsp (2 mL) each basil and oregano

❶ In saucepan, bring 4 cups (1 L) water to boil. Add potatoes, cover and cook for 8 to 10 minutes or until tender when pierced with a fork. Drain well, mash with a potato masher until fluffy, and stir in salt, pepper and olive oil.

❷ Lightly oil pie plate and spoon mashed potatoes into it. With back of spoon, spread potatoes out and top with tomato, cheese, and your choice of toppings. Sprinkle with basil and oregano and 3 or 4 drops of olive oil.

❸ Place under preheated broiler until cheese melts and pizza is piping hot.

SERVES ONE

RICE AND
BEANS

■■■■■■■■■■■■■■■■■■■■■■■■■■■■■■■■

China

ORIENTAL SHORT-GRAIN RICE
(Fan)

Most countries in southeast Asia favor short- or medium-grain rice, cooked without salt. It is nice for a change, and because it is stickier, can be eaten with chopsticks. Serve with stir-fried dishes, Meatballs in Sweet-and-Sour Sauce (page 116) or try the following simple vegetable Chop Suey.

3/4 cup (175 mL) short-grain rice
1 cup (250 mL) unsalted water

❶ Wash rice if necessary (see page 61). Put water in pot with tightly fitting lid and add rice. Bring to boil and let it bubble rapidly for 2 minutes.

❷ Cover pot, reduce heat to low and cook for 10 minutes. Do not uncover during this time. Turn heat off and let rice sit undisturbed for another 5 minutes.

CHOP SUEY

Use this recipe as a guide only. A wide variety of vegetables can be used, including Chinese cabbage, green beans, celery, broccoli, onion, bean sprouts and sugar peas.

2 tbsp (25 mL) vegetable oil (flavored with sesame oil if you have it)
1 clove garlic
2 cups (500 mL) vegetables, chopped, sliced and slivered
½ tsp (2 mL) granulated sugar

SERVES ONE OR TWO

¼ tsp (1 mL) salt
1 tbsp (15 mL) (or more) soy sauce
1 tsp (5 mL) sesame seeds (optional)

❶ Place wok or large frying pan over medium heat and pour in oil. Add garlic and cook for 2 minutes. Discard garlic and add vegetables a few at a time (the harder ones first – carrots, broccoli stems – and then the softer ones – bean sprouts, sugar peas). Stir-fry for 3 to 5 minutes or until vegetables are tender-crisp. Sprinkle with sugar and salt, drizzle with soy sauce, and spoon onto warm plate.

❷ Sprinkle with sesame seeds, if you have them.

STIR-FRYING IS VERY SIMPLE. JUST REMEMBER TO STIR CONTINUOUSLY TO ENSURE EVEN COOKING, KEEP THE PAN HOT, AND BE SURE YOUR WOK OR FRYING PAN IS LARGE ENOUGH TO HOLD THE INGREDIENTS WITHOUT OVER-CROWDING; OTHERWISE, THE FOOD WILL BE STEAMED.

■ ■

India
BASIC LONG-GRAIN RICE
(Chawal)

For many people, rice is the major part of a meal and ³⁄₄ cup (175 mL) of raw rice per person is not an unusually large portion. Serve long-grain rice with chicken, meat and curries, or try the unusual Tropical Fruit Sauce below.

³⁄₄ cup (175 mL) long-grain rice
4 to 8 cups (1 to 2 L) water
1 tbsp (15 mL) salt

❶ Wash and drain rice if necessary (see page 61).

❷ In large saucepan, bring water to rolling boil. Add salt and gradually sprinkle in rice so that the water does not stop boiling.

❸ Stir once and then boil, uncovered, for 10 to 15 minutes. Spoon out a grain and bite it. If it is still chewy but not hard in the center, it is done. Remove rice from heat and drain immediately. Mound onto warm plate and cover with a clean tea towel to keep rice hot and to allow steam to be absorbed into cloth.

TROPICAL FRUIT SAUCE

1 tbsp (15 mL) butter or vegetable oil
1 medium onion, sliced
¹⁄₂ green pepper, sliced
1 small banana, sliced
1 small apple, chopped

SERVES ONE OR TWO

2 tbsp (25 mL) raisins
1 to 2 tsp (5 to 10 mL) curry powder
½ tsp (2 mL) all-purpose flour
Juice of ½ lemon
½ cup (125 mL) water

❶ In frying pan, melt butter over medium heat. Add onion and cook for 1 minute or until translucent. Add green pepper and fruit and stir well.

❷ In a cup, mix curry powder and flour. Stir into mixture in pan. Add lemon juice and water, bring to boil and reduce heat to low. Simmer for 5 minutes or until thickened and heated through. Ladle sauce over rice.

To reheat rice cooked by this method, simply spoon into a pot of boiling water and let it cook for 5 or **6 seconds.** Drain immediately and serve on a warm plate.

■■■■■■■■■■■■■■■■■■■■■■■■■■■■■■■■

Iran
BASMATI RICE
(Chelo)

SERVES TWO

Rice is the perfect basic food. It presents no storage problems, is filling, easy to prepare and can be bought cheaply in bulk. Chelo can be served with broiled meat kebabs or chops, fried eggs or Vegetable Walnut Omelet (page 13).

3/4 cup (175 mL) basmati rice
5 to 6 cups (1.25 to 1.5 L) water
1 tbsp (15 mL) salt
2 to 3 tbsp (25 to 45 mL) butter

❶ Wash imported basmati rice. In bowl, soak rice in salted water for at least 2 hours. Drain and rinse.

❷ Bring 5 to 6 cups (1.25 to 1.5 L) water and 1 tbsp (15 mL) salt to boil, add rice and boil rapidly, uncovered, for 1 to 2 minutes. Bite a grain of rice. If it is still chewy but not hard in the center, remove rice from heat and drain immediately. Return saucepan to heat and add butter and 3 tbsp (45 mL) water.

❸ Pile drained rice into a cone shape in saucepan. Cover saucepan with a clean tea towel and lid or plate. Reduce heat to very low and steam for 10 to 15 minutes. (The cloth absorbs excess moisture, leaving rice light and fluffy.) To serve, place saucepan briefly in cold water and invert onto plate. The buttery crust on the bottom should come free.

Iꜰ sᴏᴀᴋᴇᴅ ᴏᴠᴇʀɴɪɢʜᴛ ᴏʀ ʟᴏɴɢᴇʀ, ᴋᴇᴇᴘ ᴛʜᴇ ʀɪᴄᴇ

ʀᴇꜰʀɪɢᴇʀᴀᴛᴇᴅ sᴏ ᴛʜᴀᴛ ɪᴛ ᴅᴏᴇs ɴᴏᴛ sᴛᴀʀᴛ ᴛᴏ ꜰᴇʀᴍᴇɴᴛ.

■ ■

Canada

RICE PIE CRUST

(Tarte de Riz)

This is a terrific recipe using leftover rice. It looks complicated but is easy as pie. Serve at room temperature with crisp greens and a squeeze of fresh lemon.

SERVES ONE

1½ cups (375 mL) cooked long- or short-grain rice
1 egg, beaten with a fork
¼ tsp (1 mL) each salt and tarragon (or favorite herb)
Pinch black pepper

❶ In bowl, combine rice, beaten egg, salt, tarragon and pepper, and mix thoroughly.

❷ Spoon into 8-inch (20-cm) pie plate and, with wet hands, pat into the shape of a pie crust.

❸ Bake in 450° F (230° C) oven for 5 minutes or until crust begins to brown. Remove from oven and pour in filling. Bake another 10 minutes or until filling is set and cheese has melted.

FAVORITE FILLINGS

Cheddar Cheese Filling: Mix together 1 beaten egg, ½ cup (125 mL) milk or light cream and ¾ cup (175 mL) grated cheese (Cheddar, Swiss or whatever you have).

Apple and Blue Cheese Filling: Mix together 1 beaten egg, ½ cup (125 mL) milk, 1 peeled and diced apple and ¼ cup (50 mL) crumbled blue cheese.

Onion Filling: Mix together 1 beaten egg, ½ cup (125 mL) milk and 1 cup (250 mL) fried onion slices. Season with ¼ tsp (1 mL) each salt, pepper and nutmeg.

Black Bean Filling: Mix together ¾ cup (175 mL) cooked black beans, ¼ cup (50 mL) grated mozzarella cheese and ½ tsp (2 mL) ground cumin.

Unfilled rice crusts can be frozen. Place crust in

pie plate in a sealed freezer bag and use within

one month.

■ ■

Spain

RICE WITH SAUSAGE AND TOMATO

(Arroz con Chorizo y Tomate)

This is an old-fashioned favorite brought up to date with the addition of smoked spicy sausage rather than bacon.

SERVES ONE OR TWO

1 to 2 tbsp (15 to 25 mL) olive or vegetable oil
1 medium onion, chopped
¾ cup (175 mL) short-grain rice
½ tsp (2 mL) granulated sugar
Pinch black pepper
1 cup (250 mL) whole or diced canned tomatoes,
  undrained, or
2 tbsp (25 mL) tomato paste mixed with
  1 cup (250 mL) water
½ green pepper, chopped
4 to 6 slices chorizo sausage or any smoked
  cooked sausage
¼ cup (50 mL) Spanish olives (optional)

❶ Place saucepan with a tightly fitting lid over medium heat and pour in oil. Add onion, stir and cook for 1 minute. Add rice, sugar and pepper and mix well.
❷ Stir in tomatoes with their liquid and bring to boil.
❸ Cover pan, reduce heat to low and simmer for 15 minutes. Stir in green pepper, sausage and a little more liquid if mixture seems dry. Simmer, covered, for 5 more minutes. Serve in warm soup bowl garnished with olives, if using.

RICE IMPORTED IN BURLAP SACKS AND REPACKAGED OR

SOLD IN BULK SHOULD BE WASHED.

■■■■■■■■■■■■■■■■■■■■■■■■■■■■■■■■

Indonesia
LEMON COCONUT RICE
(Nasi Uduk)

SERVES TWO

This is a very subtle and fragrant rice dish that would go well with simple grilled chicken wings and a sliced pear salad with a squeeze of lemon.

¾ **cup (175 mL) unsweetened, desiccated coconut**
1½ **cups (375 mL) boiling water**
½ **lemon, juice and grated yellow rind only**
½ **tsp (2 mL) each salt, nutmeg and ground cloves**
Pinch black pepper
¾ **cup (175 mL) long-grain rice**
1 **tbsp (15 mL) grated toasted coconut (optional)**

❶ In bowl, cover coconut with boiling water. Let cool to lukewarm, stir and crush with back of a spoon. Strain into another bowl, pressing out as much liquid as possible.

❷ In saucepan, combine coconut liquid (coconut milk), lemon juice and rind, salt, nutmeg, cloves and pepper. Bring to boil and stir in rice.

❸ Return to boil, cover and reduce heat to low. Simmer for 15 to 20 minutes. Uncover, stir gently with a fork, taking care not to crush grains, replace lid and cook for 5 minutes longer or until tender. Spoon onto warm plate and sprinkle with lightly toasted coconut.

"Coconut milk" is actually a "tea" made by straining a mixture of grated coconut and boiling water.

■ ■

Italy

RISOTTO WITH MUSHROOMS

(Risotto ai Funghi)

Mushrooms are an expensive luxury for those on a tight budget, so it is important to get full flavor for your money. This classic dish complements rather than overwhelms the delicate taste of the mushrooms.

3 tbsp (45 mL) butter 45 mL
1 small onion, thinly sliced
10 large mushrooms, cleaned and sliced thinly
3/4 cup (175 mL) short-grain rice (preferably Arborio)
2 cups (500 mL) boiling stock
¼ cup (50 mL) grated Parmesan cheese

❶ In large heavy saucepan, melt half of the butter over low heat. Add onion and cook for 3 to 4 minutes or until translucent but not brown. Stir in mushroom slices. Add rice and stir constantly, until mixture is coated with butter and rice begins to brown.

❷ Add ½ cup (125 mL) hot stock, stir and cook until it has been absorbed by the rice, then add another ½ cup (125 mL) stock. Continue adding stock in this manner until it has all been absorbed and rice is tender. This will take 15 to 20 minutes.

❸ Add Parmesan cheese and remaining butter. Gently mix together without crushing rice. Serve in soup bowl.

MUSHROOMS SHOULD NEVER BE WASHED, BUT WIPED

WITH A DAMP CLOTH. STORE IN REFRIGERATOR IN PAPER

RATHER THAN PLASTIC BAGS.

SERVES ONE OR TWO

China
GINGER FRIED RICE
(Cha'o Fan)

Cha'o Fan in China, Nasi Goreng in Indonesia, Khao Phat in Thailand, fried rice makes a fast and filling meal anywhere. Use this recipe as a guide only and choose local vegetables in season rather than more expensive foreign imports.

1 tsp (5 mL) vegetable oil
2 eggs, beaten
2 tbsp (25 mL) vegetable oil (flavored with sesame oil if you have it)
1 clove garlic, minced
1 1-inch (2.5-cm) piece fresh ginger root, peeled and grated
1 leek, or
3 green onions, sliced
1 carrot, grated, or
1 stalk celery, chopped
¼ cup (50 mL) peas or green beans
1 cup (250 mL) cooked rice
½ cup (125 mL) sliced cooked pork or chicken (optional)
2 tbsp (25 mL) soy sauce
¼ tsp (1 mL) salt
Pinch black pepper

❶ Place wok or large frying pan over medium-high heat. Add 1 tsp (5 mL) oil and beaten eggs. Cook until set and flip over like a pancake. Remove from pan and chop into small squares. Set aside.

❷ Add 2 tbsp (25 mL) oil and toss in garlic and ginger. Cook for 30 seconds. Add prepared vegetables a few at a time so that pan does not cool down. Stir-fry for 2 or 3 minutes or until vegetables are tender-crisp. Add cooked rice and meat, if using, and stir-fry for an additional 1 to 2 minutes.

❸ Season with soy sauce, salt and pepper. Spoon into bowl and top with egg.

LEEKS, OR "PAUPER'S ASPARAGUS," ARE MILDER THAN

WINTER ONIONS. THEY ARE USEFUL IN STIR-FRIED MEALS

BECAUSE THEY SLICE AND COOK QUICKLY.

Japan

SUSHI RICE WITH TOPPINGS

(Chirashi Zushi)

If you love sushi but haven't the time to roll and decorate your own, this recipe is a treasure. It has all the flavor of sushi but is served as a bowl of sweet vinegared rice topped with favorite ingredients.

SERVES ONE

Rice

3 tbsp (45 mL) rice vinegar or mild white vinegar
1 tbsp (15 mL) granulated sugar
½ tsp (2 mL) salt
1½ cups (375 mL) hot cooked Oriental Short-Grain Rice (page 54)

Toppings

There are no hard and fast rules; choose whatever is available with an eye to color and texture. Suggestions include:

1 sheet nori (dried seaweed), sliced
2 tbsp (25 mL) cucumber, diced
¼ cup (50 mL) cooked green peas
1 egg omelet, sliced (page 14)
1 or 2 dried mushrooms (see note below)
½ avocado, peeled and diced
1 imitation crab stick or sea leg
¼ cup (50 mL) sliced, fresh fish
¼ cup (50 mL) diced, fried tofu

3 green onions, chopped
Soy sauce to taste

❶ In cup, mix together vinegar, sugar and salt. Stir until sugar is completely dissolved.

❷ Place hot cooked rice in bowl and pour vinegar mixture over top. Mix gently but thoroughly and let cool to room temperature. Top with your choice of toppings.

❸ Serve in the bowl and season with soy sauce.

To reconstitute dried mushrooms, rinse in cold water then soak in boiling water for **15** minutes. After soaking, slice mushrooms and either sauté them in butter or simmer them for **5** minutes in water flavored with soy sauce.

■ ■

Italy

RICE CAKES WITH MOZZARELLA
(Arancini di Riso)

I first tasted these fabulous rice and cheese cakes thirty years ago while crossing the Straits of Messina between Italy and Sicily. They were round like little oranges and deep-fried to a golden brown. I like to pan-fry them and serve with a rich Tomato Sauce (page 146).

SERVES ONE

2 cups (500 mL) Basic Meat Stock (page 26)
¾ cup (175 mL) short-grain rice (preferably Arborio)
1 tbsp (15 mL) butter
3 to 4 tbsp (45 to 60 mL) grated Parmesan cheese
1 egg, beaten
½ tsp (2 mL) each basil and oregano
Salt and pepper to taste
6 cubes (sugar lump size) mozzarella cheese
¾ cup (175 mL) dry bread crumbs
4 tbsp (60 mL) vegetable oil
Tomato Sauce (page 146)

❶ In medium saucepan, bring stock to rolling boil. Stir in rice and bring back to boil. Cover pan, reduce heat to medium and simmer for 15 minutes or until rice is tender. Stir in butter, cheese, beaten egg, basil, oregano, salt and pepper and mix well.

❷ Spread rice mixture on plate to cool slightly. With wet hands, shape into 6 balls. Plunge thumb into middle of each ball, making a hollow for cube of cheese. Place cheese cube into each hollow, cover holes with rice mixture and roll balls in bread crumbs. Flatten balls with palm of your hand.

❸ Place frying pan over medium heat and pour in oil. Add cakes and pan-fry for 2 to 3 minutes on each side until outside is crisp and golden and cheese on the inside has melted. Drain cakes on paper towel.

SHORT-GRAIN BROWN RICE CAN BE SUBSTITUTED, BUT IT TAKES LONGER TO COOK THAN WHITE RICE. SOME VARI-TIES NEED TO SIMMER FOR 30 TO 40 MINUTES. FOLLOW PACKAGE INSTRUCTIONS FOR EXACT COOKING TIMES.

■■■■■■■■■■■■■■■■■■■■■■■■■■■■■■

Turkey
SPICY GOLDEN PILAF
(Iç Pilav)

This spicy and aromatic mixture of rice, fruit, nuts and vegetables makes a filling dinner for very little cost. It is delicious on its own or as an accompaniment to a simple broiled lamb chop or chicken wings.

SERVES ONE OR TWO

¾ cup (175 mL) long-grain rice
2 to 3 tbsp (25 to 45 mL) butter
1 medium onion, chopped
1 clove garlic, minced
½ tsp (2 mL) each allspice, cinnamon, turmeric and nutmeg
¼ tsp (1 mL) each salt and pepper or to taste
1½ cups (375 mL) Basic Meat Stock (page 26) or vegetable stock
2 to 3 (25 to 45 mL) tbsp pine nuts or walnuts
2 tbsp (25 mL) currants, dried apricots or raisins

❶ Wash rice, if necessary (see page 61), and drain until dry.

❷ In heavy saucepan, melt butter over medium heat. Add onion and garlic and cook for 2 to 3 minutes or until translucent. Add rice and stir until mixture is coated with butter and rice is beginning to brown, about 2 minutes.

❸ Stir spices, salt and pepper into stock and add to rice mixture with nuts and fruit. Bring to boil, cover and reduce heat to low. Simmer for 10 to 12 minutes or until liquid is absorbed. Turn heat off. Remove lid, place clean tea towel and a plate over saucepan, and let stand for another 5 minutes. (Excess moisture will be absorbed by towel). Fluff with a fork and spoon onto warm plate.

TURMERIC HAS BEEN CALLED "POOR MAN'S SAFFRON."

IT GIVES RICE AND SAUCES THE BRILLIANT GOLDEN

YELLOW COLOR WITHOUT, ALAS, THE AROMA.

■ ■

Cuba
RICE AND BEANS
(Moros y Cristianos)

SERVES ONE

If you have never tried black beans, you are missing a delicious Cuban staple dish. Black beans are also good cold in mixed vegetable salads. Dried beans must be soaked overnight and then simmered for 2 hours before using. About ½ cup (125 mL) of dried beans will yield 1 cup (250 mL) of cooked beans. They can also be bought in cans, ready to heat.

2 tbsp (25 mL) vegetable oil
1 medium onion, chopped
1 clove garlic, crushed
2 slices bacon, chopped
½ green pepper, chopped
1 tomato, chopped
½ cup (125 mL) water
½ tsp (2 mL) granulated sugar
Salt and pepper to taste
1 cup (250 mL) cooked black beans
1 tsp (5 mL) ground cumin or chili powder
1 tbsp (15 mL) apple cider vinegar (or another mild vinegar)
1 cup (250 mL) hot cooked white rice

❶ Place frying pan over medium heat and pour in oil. Add onion, garlic, bacon and green pepper and cook for 5 minutes, stirring occasionally. Add tomato, water, sugar, salt and pepper. Cook only until hot and bubbling.

❷ Gently stir in cooked black beans, cumin and vinegar. Reduce heat to low, cover and simmer for 5 to 8 minutes.

❸ Spoon rice into center of plate and top with bean mixture.

■ ■

Saudi Arabia
BEAN BURGERS
(Falafel)

A cross between a pancake and a burger, these delicious cakes are crunchy on the outside and soft in the middle. They are popular served like a sandwich inside pita bread or as a main dish with tomato salad dressed with yogurt.

SERVES ONE

1 cup (250 mL) cooked chick-peas
1 clove garlic, minced
2 green onions, finely chopped
½ tsp (2 mL) salt
½ tsp (2 mL) baking powder
¼ tsp (1 mL) each ground cumin and ground
　coriander
2 drops Tabasco sauce
1 egg, beaten
¼ cup (50 mL) all-purpose flour
2 to 3 (25 to 45 mL) tbsp vegetable oil

❶ Drain and mash chick-peas with a potato masher. Add garlic, green onions, salt, baking powder, cumin, coriander and Tabasco sauce and mix thoroughly.

❷ Stir in beaten egg. With wet hands, form 3 patties. Dredge in flour on both sides, turning with spatula.

❸ Place frying pan over medium heat and pour in oil. Pan-fry patties on each side for 3 to 4 minutes or until they are crisp and brown on the outside and hot through.

■■■■■■■■■■■■■■■■■■■■■■■■■■■■■■

Mexico
REFRIED BEANS
(Frijoles Refritos)

Refried beans are simple to make and taste so much better than those in a can. I like mine spicy with cumin and coriander and lots of garlic. They are great as a filling for burritos or on their own with a few chunks of chorizo sausage, Quick Homemade Salsa (page 8) and tortilla chips. Soak dried pinto beans for 2 to 3 hours. Drain and place in a saucepan, cover with water and simmer, covered, for about 45 minutes.

1½ cups (375 mL) cooked pinto beans, drained
⅓ cup (75 mL) water
4 tbsp (60 mL) vegetable oil
2 or 3 cloves garlic, crushed
1 small onion, sliced
½ tsp (2 mL) each ground cumin and ground
   coriander
Salt and pepper to taste
½ cup (125 mL) grated white cheese (farmer's,
   brick or Cheddar)

❶ In bowl, mash pinto beans and water with a potato masher. Beans should be chunky, not smooth.
❷ Place frying pan over medium-low heat. Pour in oil and stir in garlic, onion, cumin, coriander, salt and pepper. Stir and cook for 1 to 2 minutes or until onion is translucent. Add mashed beans and cook gently, stirring continuously, for 8 to 10 minutes or until mixture is hot and flavors have melded.
❸ Add cheese, stir gently just until cheese has melted and serve on warm plate.

■■■■■■■■■■■■■■■■■■■■■■■■■■■■■■

India

GINGER CHICK-PEAS

(Kabli Channas)

This inexpensive dish of chick-peas cooked in richly seasoned stock and enhanced with exotic spices is delicious. Pour over hot cooked rice or serve in a bowl with garlic toast. Canned cooked chick peas are readily available, and are great in mixed salads, pasta or soup. A 19-oz (540 mL) can, when drained, yields 2 cups (500 mL).

S E R V E S   O N E   O R   T W O

2 tbsp (25 mL) butter or vegetable oil
1 medium onion, chopped
2 cloves garlic
1 ½-inch (1-cm) piece fresh ginger root, peeled
  and shredded
½ tsp (2 mL) each turmeric and salt
¼ tsp (1 mL) each ground cloves, ground cumin
  and cinnamon
Pinch cayenne pepper, or
1 or 2 drops Tabasco sauce
2 tomatoes, chopped
1½ cups (375 mL) cooked chick-peas, drained
¾ cup (175 mL) Basic Meat Stock (page 61) or
  vegetable stock

❶ In frying pan, melt butter over medium heat. Cook onion and garlic for 2 minutes or until translucent. Stir in ginger, turmeric, salt, spices and cayenne pepper.

❷ Add tomatoes, chick-peas and stock and bring to boil, stirring continuously.

❸ Cover, reduce heat to low and simmer gently for 10 minutes.

■■■■■■■■■■■■■■■■■■■■■■■■■■■■■■■■

Italy

BEANS AND SAUSAGE ON SPINACH SALAD

(Fagioli con le Cotechino)

Early spring spinach is so tender that it needs no cooking. Dress with warm beans and slices of spicy Italian sausage for a quick and unusual supper dish.

SERVES ONE

1 or 2 hot or mild Italian sausages
1 tbsp (15 mL) vegetable oil
1 small onion, thinly sliced
½ green pepper, sliced
½ cup (125 mL) cooked white beans, drained
½ cup (125 mL) red wine or unsweetened
  fruit juice
¼ tsp (1 mL) each thyme and sage
Salt and pepper to taste
1½ cups (375 mL) spinach, washed and dried

❶ Place frying pan over medium-low heat and pour in oil. Add sausages and cook, turning repeatedly, until they are browned and cooked through, about 10 to 15 minutes. Remove from pan and thinly slice.

❷ Remove all but 1 tbsp (15 mL) fat from pan. Increase heat to medium and toss in onion and green pepper. Stir and cook vegetables for 3 to 4 minutes or until tender but still crisp. Add sliced sausage, beans, wine, thyme, sage, salt and pepper and bring to boil. Reduce heat to low and let mixture bubble gently until heated through.

❸ Tear spinach into bite-sized pieces and place on plate. Top with hot bean and sausage mixture.

■■■■■■■■■■■■■■■■■■■■■■■■■■■■■■■

Turkey
BYZANTINE BEANS
(Fasulye Pilaki)

This is a really simple mixture of beans and veggies in a sweet tomato sauce, but it is delicious. Serve hot or Turkish style at room temperature with wedges of lemon and Ekmek or French bread.

2 to 3 tbsp (25 to 45 mL) vegetable oil
1 small onion, chopped
1 medium carrot, scrubbed and chopped
½ cup (125 mL) cooked white kidney beans, drained
1 potato, peeled and cubed (size of sugar cubes)
1 clove garlic, crushed
⅔ to 1 cup (150 to 250 mL) hot water
1 tbsp (15 mL) tomato paste
1 tsp (5 mL) granulated sugar
½ tsp (2 mL) salt
1 lemon wedge
Fresh parsley sprigs

❶ Place frying pan over medium heat and pour in oil. Add onion and cook for 2 to 3 minutes or until translucent.

❷ Stir in carrot, beans, potato, garlic, ½ cup (125 mL) water, tomato paste, sugar and salt and bring to boil. Reduce heat to low, cover and cook for 15 to 20 minutes.

❸ Uncover pan and stir in more water if it seems dry. Re-cover pan and gently simmer for 2 more minutes or until vegetables are soft. Serve in bowl garnished with lemon wedge and parsley.

S E R V E S   O N E

WHITE KIDNEY OR CANNELLINI BEANS CAN BE BOUGHT READY-COOKED AND CANNED. IF YOU HAVE EXTRA TIME SOAK AND COOK A LARGE QUANTITY OF DRIED BEANS. THEY CAN BE PACKAGED IN SINGLE-SIZED PORTIONS IN REUSABLE PLASTIC FREEZER BAGS, SEALED AND FROZEN.

FISH

■■■■■■■■■■■■■■■■■■■■■■■■■■■■■■

China

SWEET-AND-SOUR SNAPPER

(Jeung Yue)

This delicately flavored sweet -and-sour sauce enhances the taste of fresh snapper. Serve with Oriental Short Grain Rice (page 54) and sliced cucumber salad.

1 4- to 6-oz (125- to 170-g) snapper fillet
2 tbsp (25 mL) soy sauce
1 to 2 tbsp (15 to 25 mL) vegetable oil (flavored
   with sesame oil if you have it)
1 clove garlic, crushed
¾ cup (175 mL) vegetable stock or water

....

Sᴡᴇᴇᴛ-ᴀɴᴅ-Sᴏᴜʀ Sᴀᴜᴄᴇ

1 tsp (5 mL) cornstarch
2 tbsp (25 mL) white or apple cider vinegar
1 tbsp (15 mL) brown or granulated sugar
1 tbsp (15 mL) soy sauce
1 ½-inch (1-cm) piece fresh ginger root, peeled
   and grated

❶ Make several 2-inch (5-cm) gashes along one side of fillet and brush with soy sauce.

❷ Place frying pan over medium-high heat and pour in oil. Add garlic and cook for 1 minute. Remove and discard. Place fillet in garlic-flavored oil and cook for 2 minutes on each side or until golden brown. Pour stock over fish, cover, reduce heat to low and simmer for 5 minutes or until fish is tender. Remove from pan with spatula, place on plate and cover with pot lid to keep warm.

❸ In small bowl, mix sauce ingredients until smooth. Add to pan with fish juices and bring to boil, stirring vigorously. Sauce will thicken slightly in 30 seconds. Pour sauce over fish.

BEFORE CORNSTARCH CAN BE ADDED TO HOT INGREDI-

ENTS, IT MUST FIRST BE MIXED WITH A COLD LIQUID TO

PREVENT LUMPS FROM FORMING.

■ ■

Portugal
FRESH COD WITH GREEN PEAS
(Pescado à Portugũesa)

This is a simple dish that dresses up the mildest piece of cod with color and zest. Serve with boiled new potatoes or Parmesan Potato Wedges (page 50).

SERVES ONE

1 4- to 6-oz (125- to 170-g) cod fillet or any firm
  white fish
¼ tsp (1 mL) each salt and pepper
2 tbsp (25 mL) vegetable oil
1 small onion, thinly sliced
1 clove garlic, minced
1 tomato, chopped
¼ cup (50 mL) hot water
½ tsp (2 mL) granulated sugar
¼ tsp (1 mL) salt
Pinch black pepper
½ cup (125 mL) green peas, thawed

❶ Sprinkle fish fillet with salt and pepper and place in oiled baking dish.

❷ Place small pot over medium heat and pour in oil. Add onion and garlic and cook for 1 to 2 minutes or until onion is translucent. Stir in tomato, hot water, sugar, salt and pepper and bring to boil.

❸ Immediately pour mixture over fish and bake, uncovered, in preheated 400°F (200° C) oven for 10 minutes. Add peas and continue baking for another 5 minutes or until peas are heated through and fish is opaque. Serve on warm plate.

To remove the odor of fish from cooking utensils and hands, rinse in vinegar and water.

■ ■

Greece

FISH WITH LEMON HERB CRUST

(Psári Plakí)

Snapper or cod fillets are baked with a lively mixture of vegetables, oregano and lemon zest. Delicious served with orzo or another small pasta.

SERVES ONE

2 tbsp (25 mL) oil (preferably olive oil)
1 clove garlic, minced
1 small onion, chopped
½ green pepper, sliced
1 tomato, chopped
¼ cup (50 mL) chopped fresh parsley
½ tsp (2 mL) oregano
Salt and pepper to taste
1 4- to 6-oz (125- to 170-g) snapper or cod fillet
1 lemon, juice and grated rind (yellow skin only)
½ cup (125 mL) croutons or dry bread crumbs
¼ cup (50 mL) tomato juice, or
1 tsp (5 mL) tomato paste and water

❶ Place frying pan over medium heat and pour in oil. Add garlic, onion and pepper, and cook for 1 to 2 minutes or until onion is translucent. Stir in tomato and cook for another minute. Add parsley, oregano, salt and pepper. Mix well and remove from heat.

❷ Put fish in oiled pie plate. Spoon vegetable mixture on top and sprinkle with lemon zest and croutons.

❸ Mix tomato and lemon juices together. Pour over fish and bake, uncovered, in 425° F (220° C) oven for 15 to 20 minutes or until fish is cooked.

■■■■■■■■■■■■■■■■■■■■■■■■■■■■■■■

India
SPICY FISH CAKES
(Machi Kabab)

These crispy fried cakes with a hint of ginger are a delicious way to use up leftovers or to stretch a small amount of canned fish into a meal. Serve with a grated carrot salad.

SERVES ONE

4 oz (125 g) cooked fish (canned or freshly cooked), drained
½ cup (125 mL) cooked diced or mashed potatoes
½ cup (125 mL) dry bread crumbs or cracker crumbs
2 tbsp (25 mL) grated onion
1 tsp (5 mL) finely chopped green chili pepper
1 egg, beaten lightly with a fork
1 ½-inch (1-cm) piece fresh ginger root, peeled and shredded
¼ tsp (1 mL) each salt and pepper
1 tbsp (15 mL) each vegetable oil and butter
Lemon wedges

❶ In bowl, flake fish with a fork. Stir in potatoes, bread crumbs, onion and chili pepper, and mix well. Add beaten egg to bind mixture together. Season with ginger, salt and pepper.

❷ With floured hands, form mixture into cakes about ½ inch (1 cm) thick.

❸ Combine oil and butter in frying pan over medium-high heat. Add fish cakes in a single layer and cook until crispy and golden brown, about 3 to 4 minutes on each side. Serve on warm plate with wedges of lemon.

■■■■■■■■■■■■■■■■■■■■■■■■■■■■■■■

Barbados
FLYING FISH IN BREAD CRUMBS

Fresh cod and snapper, spiced with allspice, thyme and hot cayenne pepper, are excellent substitutes for the remarkable flying fish of Barbados. Serve with hot rice and a sliced lime or lemon.

S
E
R
V
E
S

O
N
E

1 egg
1 tbsp (15 mL) water
½ tsp (2 mL) allspice or nutmeg
½ tsp (2 mL) thyme
Pinch cayenne pepper
¼ tsp (1 mL) salt
1 4- to 6-oz (125- to 170-g) flying fish, cod or
   snapper fillet
½ cup (125 mL) dry bread crumbs
2 to 3 tbsp (25 to 45 mL) vegetable oil

❶ In flat dish or pie plate, beat together egg, water and seasonings. Dip fish into egg mixture then press into bread crumbs. Repeat using up egg mixture and crumbs.

❷ Place frying pan over medium-high heat and pour in oil. Pan-fry fillet until golden brown on both sides. Reduce heat to low and cook until fish is tender. Allow 10 minutes for a 1-inch (2.5-cm) thick fillet.

❸ Drain fillet on paper towel and place on warm plate.

LIKE LITTLE BIRDS, FLYING FISH SKIM ALONG THE WATER

THEN PROPEL THEMSELVES INTO THE AIR AND "FLY" FOR

AMAZING DISTANCES.

■■■■■■■■■■■■■■■■■■■■■■■■■■■■■■

Italy

GRILLED FISH AND PEPPERS

(Pesce in Graticola)

SERVES ONE

*Garlic and lemon permeate this colorful seafood and veg-
etable grill. Choose any fresh or saltwater fish that is available at a good price. Serve with rice or potatoes.*

**1 4- to 6-oz (125- to 170-g) fish fillet (cod,
    snapper, halibut)**
4 tbsp (60 mL) olive oil or vegetable oil
½ lemon, juice and 1 slice
2 cloves garlic, minced
¼ tsp (1 mL) each salt and pepper
2 tbsp (25 mL) minced fresh parsley
3 cherry tomatoes
1 green or yellow pepper, sliced

❶ Slash fillet in the thickest part so it will cook evenly.

❷ In flat dish or pie plate, mix together oil, lemon
juice, garlic, salt, pepper and parsley. Marinate fish
and vegetables in oil mixture for up to 30 minutes,
depending upon how much time you have. Allow
10 minutes to preheat oven broiler.

❸ Remove fish and vegetables from marinade and
place on oiled broiler pan. Top fish with thin slice of
lemon. Put in oven 6 inches (15 cm) from heat and
broil for 5 to 6 minutes per side, or until fish is
cooked, occasionally brushing with marinade.

IF USING A BARBECUE, GRILL FISH ABOUT 4 INCHES

(10 CM) ABOVE HOT COALS.

■■■■■■■■■■■■■■■■■■■■■■■■■■■■■■■■

Canada
FISH BAKED WITH CREAM CHEESE

The origin of this colorful and unusual family favorite is a bit of a mystery. It looks far more complicated than it really is and stretches a small amount of fish into a rich and filling entrée.

SERVES ONE

1 4- to 6-oz (125- to 170-g) cod or other white
  fish fillet
2 to 3 tbsp (25 to 45 mL) cream cheese
1 tbsp (15 mL) mayonnaise
1 small carrot, grated
1 small tomato, chopped
3 green onions, chopped
1 sprig fresh parsley, chopped
Salt and pepper to taste
Cooked spinach

❶ Preheat oven to 400° F (200° C). Place fillet in oiled baking dish.

❷ In small bowl, mix together cream cheese, mayonnaise, vegetables and seasoning with a fork.

❸ Spoon cream cheese mixture on top of fillet, smoothing top with a knife.

❹ Bake, uncovered, for about 15 minutes or until fish flakes easily with a fork and top is slightly golden. Serve on a bed of spinach or other green vegetable.

■ ■

England
SIMPLE POACHED FISH

A perfect foil for the delicious sauces found on the next page. Leftovers can be used cold in salads, tossed into hot pasta, or made into Spicy Fish Cakes (page 84) or fillings for toasted sandwiches.

1 tbsp (15 mL) white vinegar
½ tsp (2 ml) salt
1 8-oz (250-g) fish steak
Sliced cucumber and tomato, or Sauce for Fish (page 89)

❶ In saucepan, bring 2 inches (5 cm) water to a rolling boil. Add vinegar and salt and reduce heat to simmer.

❷ Lower steak into simmering water, cover and gently simmer (never boil) for 8 to 10 minutes or until fish flakes easily with a fork.

❸ Remove from pan with spatula, drain well and place on warm plate. Garnish with cucumber, tomato or one of the sauces on the following pages.

TO COOK A WHOLE FISH IN A LARGE ROASTING PAN, USE

ENOUGH BOILING LIQUID TO COMPLETELY COVER. THE

GENERAL RULE FOR TIMING IS 10 MINUTES PER INCH

(2.5 CM) OF FISH, MEASURED AT THE THICKEST PART.

TO CHECK THAT FISH IS COOKED, INSERT A FORK CLOSE

TO THE BACKBONE, PRESS GENTLY AND IF THE JUICES RUN

CLEAR, IT IS DONE.

SERVES ONE

■ ■

Barbados
FLYING FISH IN BREAD CRUMBS

Fresh cod and snapper, spiced with allspice, thyme and hot cayenne pepper, are excellent substitutes for the remarkable flying fish of Barbados. Serve with hot rice and a sliced lime or lemon.

SERVES ONE

1 egg
1 tbsp (15 mL) water
½ tsp (2 mL) allspice or nutmeg
½ tsp (2 mL) thyme
Pinch cayenne pepper
¼ tsp (1 mL) salt
1 4- to 6-oz (125- to 170-g) flying fish, cod or snapper fillet
½ cup (125 mL) dry bread crumbs
2 to 3 tbsp (25 to 45 mL) vegetable oil

❶ In flat dish or pie plate, beat together egg, water and seasonings. Dip fish into egg mixture then press into bread crumbs. Repeat using up egg mixture and crumbs.

❷ Place frying pan over medium-high heat and pour in oil. Pan-fry fillet until golden brown on both sides. Reduce heat to low and cook until fish is tender. Allow 10 minutes for a 1-inch (2.5-cm) thick fillet.

❸ Drain fillet on paper towel and place on warm plate.

LIKE LITTLE BIRDS, FLYING FISH SKIM ALONG THE WATER

THEN PROPEL THEMSELVES INTO THE AIR AND "FLY" FOR

AMAZING DISTANCES.

■■■■■■■■■■■■■■■■■■■■■■■■■■■■■■■

Italy
GRILLED FISH AND PEPPERS
(Pesce in Graticola)

SERVES ONE

Garlic and lemon permeate this colorful seafood and vegetable grill. Choose any fresh or saltwater fish that is available at a good price. Serve with rice or potatoes.

1 4- to 6-oz (125- to 170-g) fish fillet (cod,
   snapper, halibut)
4 tbsp (60 mL) olive oil or vegetable oil
½ lemon, juice and 1 slice
2 cloves garlic, minced
¼ tsp (1 mL) each salt and pepper
2 tbsp (25 mL) minced fresh parsley
3 cherry tomatoes
1 green or yellow pepper, sliced

❶ Slash fillet in the thickest part so it will cook evenly.

❷ In flat dish or pie plate, mix together oil, lemon juice, garlic, salt, pepper and parsley. Marinate fish and vegetables in oil mixture for up to 30 minutes, depending upon how much time you have. Allow 10 minutes to preheat oven broiler.

❸ Remove fish and vegetables from marinade and place on oiled broiler pan. Top fish with thin slice of lemon. Put in oven 6 inches (15 cm) from heat and broil for 5 to 6 minutes per side, or until fish is cooked, occasionally brushing with marinade.

Iꜰ ᴜsɪɴɢ ᴀ ʙᴀʀʙᴇᴄᴜᴇ, ɢʀɪʟʟ ꜰɪsʜ ᴀʙᴏᴜᴛ **4** ɪɴᴄʜᴇs

(10 ᴄᴍ) ᴀʙᴏᴠᴇ ʜᴏᴛ ᴄᴏᴀʟs.

▪▪▪▪▪▪▪▪▪▪▪▪▪▪▪▪▪▪▪▪▪▪▪▪▪▪▪▪▪▪▪

Canada
FISH BAKED WITH CREAM CHEESE

The origin of this colorful and unusual family favorite is a bit of a mystery. It looks far more complicated than it really is and stretches a small amount of fish into a rich and filling entrée.

S E R V E S   O N E

1 4- to 6-oz (125- to 170-g) cod or other white fish fillet
2 to 3 tbsp (25 to 45 mL) cream cheese
1 tbsp (15 mL) mayonnaise
1 small carrot, grated
1 small tomato, chopped
3 green onions, chopped
1 sprig fresh parsley, chopped
Salt and pepper to taste
Cooked spinach

❶ Preheat oven to 400° F (200° C). Place fillet in oiled baking dish.

❷ In small bowl, mix together cream cheese, mayonnaise, vegetables and seasoning with a fork.

❸ Spoon cream cheese mixture on top of fillet, smoothing top with a knife.

❹ Bake, uncovered, for about 15 minutes or until fish flakes easily with a fork and top is slightly golden. Serve on a bed of spinach or other green vegetable.

■ ■

England

SIMPLE POACHED FISH

A perfect foil for the delicious sauces found on the next page. Leftovers can be used cold in salads, tossed into hot pasta, or made into Spicy Fish Cakes (page 84) or fillings for toasted sandwiches.

1 tbsp (15 mL) white vinegar
½ tsp (2 ml) salt
1 8-oz (250-g) fish steak
Sliced cucumber and tomato, or Sauce for Fish (page 89)

❶ In saucepan, bring 2 inches (5 cm) water to a rolling boil. Add vinegar and salt and reduce heat to simmer.

❷ Lower steak into simmering water, cover and gently simmer (never boil) for 8 to 10 minutes or until fish flakes easily with a fork.

❸ Remove from pan with spatula, drain well and place on warm plate. Garnish with cucumber, tomato or one of the sauces on the following pages.

Tᴏ ᴄᴏᴏᴋ ᴀ ᴡʜᴏʟᴇ ꜰɪsʜ ɪɴ ᴀ ʟᴀʀɢᴇ ʀᴏᴀsᴛɪɴɢ ᴘᴀɴ, ᴜsᴇ ᴇɴᴏᴜɢʜ ʙᴏɪʟɪɴɢ ʟɪQᴜɪᴅ ᴛᴏ ᴄᴏᴍᴘʟᴇᴛᴇʟʏ ᴄᴏᴠᴇʀ. Tʜᴇ ɢᴇɴᴇʀᴀʟ ʀᴜʟᴇ ꜰᴏʀ ᴛɪᴍɪɴɢ ɪs 10 ᴍɪɴᴜᴛᴇs ᴘᴇʀ ɪɴᴄʜ (2.5 ᴄᴍ) ᴏꜰ ꜰɪsʜ, ᴍᴇᴀsᴜʀᴇᴅ ᴀᴛ ᴛʜᴇ ᴛʜɪᴄᴋᴇsᴛ ᴘᴀʀᴛ. Tᴏ ᴄʜᴇᴄᴋ ᴛʜᴀᴛ ꜰɪsʜ ɪs ᴄᴏᴏᴋᴇᴅ, ɪɴsᴇʀᴛ ᴀ ꜰᴏʀᴋ ᴄʟᴏsᴇ ᴛᴏ ᴛʜᴇ ʙᴀᴄᴋʙᴏɴᴇ, ᴘʀᴇss ɢᴇɴᴛʟʏ ᴀɴᴅ ɪꜰ ᴛʜᴇ ᴊᴜɪᴄᴇs ʀᴜɴ ᴄʟᴇᴀʀ, ɪᴛ ɪs ᴅᴏɴᴇ.

SERVES ONE

SAUCES FOR FISH

*Use these combinations as a guide only. Create your own
sauces with ingredients at hand and serve with fried, grilled
or poached fish. Recipes make approximately 1 cup (250 mL).
Store in a covered jar in the refrigerator.*

PARMESAN LEMON MAYONNAISE

Blend:
¾ cup (175 mL) mayonnaise
3 tbsp (45 mL) sour cream
1 tbsp (15 mL) white wine vinegar or other
   mild vinegar
1 tsp (5 mL) fresh lemon juice
Dash Worcestershire sauce
1 clove garlic, minced
1 tbsp (15 mL) finely minced onion
1 tbsp (15 mL) Parmesan cheese
1 tsp (5 mL) dillweed

GARLIC MAYONNAISE (AIOLI SAUCE)

*Traditionally served with cod. The amount of garlic used is a
matter of preference.*

Blend:
1 cup (250 mL) mayonnaise
4 or 5 cloves garlic, minced

Sauce Tartare

Blend:

¾ cup (175 mL) mayonnaise

1 tbsp (15 mL) each chopped fresh parsley,
green onions and whole capers

1 or 2 chopped sweet pickles

1 tbsp (15 mL) apple cider vinegar or other
mild vinegar

1 tsp (5 mL) caper juice

CHICKEN

■ ■

Italy

BREADED CHICKEN BREAST

(Filetto di Pollo Fritto)

*A crisp coating of bread crumbs seals in moistness and flavor.
Serve with buttered noodles or a simple pasta such as
Spaghetti with Olive Oil, Garlic and Hot Chili Pepper
(page 136).*

SERVES ONE

1 chicken breast, cut into 2 pieces
1 tsp (5 mL) each tarragon and oregano
¼ tsp (1 mL) salt
Pinch black pepper
1 tbsp (15 mL) all-purpose flour
1 egg, beaten with a fork
¾ cup (175 mL) dry bread crumbs
3 to 4 tbsp (45 to 60 mL) vegetable oil
1 tomato, sliced (optional)

❶ Rinse and dry chicken pieces and flatten with the
palm of your hand.

❷ Sprinkle chicken with herbs, salt, pepper and
flour. Dip in beaten egg then bread crumbs. Repeat
until you have a thick coating.

❸ Place ovenproof frying pan over medium heat and
pour in oil. When oil is hot, add chicken and sauté for
3 to 5 minutes per side. Once coating is sealed on
both sides, either reduce heat to low and cook for
another 10 minutes or place in 350° F (180° C) oven
and cook for another 10 minutes or until breast is
tender and no longer pink inside. Serve on warm
plate and garnish with sliced tomato, if desired.

■ ■

France

GLAZED CHICKEN

(Poulet Sautée au Vinaigre)

This is a simple but delicious way to serve chicken. Perfect Mashed Potatoes (page 48) and a green vegetable would be good accompaniments.

2 tbsp (25 mL) vegetable oil
1 chicken breast or leg with thigh attached
1 tbsp (15 mL) all-purpose flour
Pinch each salt and pepper
4 tbsp (60 mL) white wine vinegar
1 tbsp (15 mL) butter

❶ Place frying pan over medium heat and pour in oil.

❷ Dust chicken breast or leg with flour, salt and pepper. Brown on both sides in hot oil, about 4 to 5 minutes per side. Cover pan, reduce heat to medium-low and cook for another 10 minutes or until chicken is tender and no longer pink inside.

❸ Remove chicken from pan, place on plate and cover with lid to keep warm. Pour off and discard all but 2 tbsp (25 mL) of pan juices. Increase heat to medium-high, stir in vinegar and boil to reduce by half.

❹ Remove pan from heat and immediately stir butter into hot vinegar. Pour over chicken.

CHICKEN LEGS AND THIGHS TAKE LONGER TO COOK THAN BREASTS. IF COOKING DIFFERENT CHICKEN PARTS IN THE SAME PAN, REMOVE THE BREAST WHEN TENDER AND KEEP IN A WARM OVEN UNTIL THE LEGS AND THIGHS ARE COOKED.

SERVES ONE

■ ■

Azerbaijan
CHICKEN WITH PEACHES
(Persik)

*The hint of cinnamon with butter makes this dish unforget-
table. I like to serve it with Basmati Rice (page 58) to soak
up the wonderful sauce.*

S E R V E S   O N E

1 to 2 tbsp (15 to 25 mL) butter
1 chicken breast or leg
 Salt and pepper to taste
1 medium onion, chopped
2 canned peach halves, sliced
½ cup (125 mL) peach juice
½ lemon, juice and grated rind (yellow skin only)
½ tsp (2 mL) cinnamon

❶ In frying pan, melt butter over medium heat.

❷ Sprinkle chicken with salt and pepper, and sauté
on both sides until golden brown, about 3 minutes
per side. Push to one side of pan and add onion.
Cook, stirring constantly, for 2 to 3 minutes or until
onion is translucent.

❸ Spoon onion over chicken and top with peach
slices. Pour peach and lemon juices over chicken and
sprinkle with grated lemon rind and cinnamon.

❹ Cover tightly, reduce heat to low and simmer for
10 minutes or until chicken is tender and no longer
pink inside. Place chicken on warm plate, arrange
peach slices and onion on top, and ladle sauce over all.

■ ■

Mexico
CHICKEN WITH ORANGES
(Pollo con Naranjas)

Rosemary and orange are perfect flavors with chicken. Try a colorful accompaniment of hot shredded carrots and rice.

1 chicken breast or leg with thigh attached
½ tsp (2 mL) dried rosemary, crushed
¼ tsp (1 mL) salt
Pinch pepper
2 tbsp (25 mL) vegetable oil (flavored with olive oil)
½ orange, sliced
Juice of 1½ oranges

❶ Rinse and dry chicken and season with rosemary, salt and pepper.

❷ Place frying pan over medium-high heat and pour in oil. When oil is hot, add chicken and sauté on both sides for 3 to 5 minutes per side or until golden brown.

❸ Place orange slices on top and pour in juice. Cover tightly and reduce heat to low. Simmer, basting from time to time, for 10 to 15 minutes or until chicken is tender and no longer pink inside.

❹ Place chicken on warm plate and spoon a little orange sauce on top.

SERVES ONE

"FAMILY PACKS" OF FRESH CHICKEN LEGS WITH THE THIGHS ATTACHED ARE OFTEN VERY REASONABLY PRICED. REPACKAGE ONE-SERVING AMOUNTS IN SMALL FREEZER BAGS. MAKE SURE THAT THE FAMILY PACK IS NOT LABELED **PREVIOUSLY FROZEN**. IT IS NOT SAFE TO RE-FREEZE THAWED FOOD.

■ ■

China
CHICKEN BROCCOLI STIR-FRY
(Gai)

This quickly cooked stir-fry or ch'ao has a crunchy, crisp texture and fresh ginger flavor. Serve over noodles flavored with a little soy sauce and sesame oil.

1 4- to 6-oz (125- to 170-g) boneless, skinless
   chicken breast, diced
1 tsp (5 mL) cornstarch
1 tbsp (15 mL) cold water
1 tbsp (15 mL) light soy sauce
½ tsp (2 mL) granulated sugar
2 to 3 tbsp (25 to 45 mL) vegetable oil
1 cup (250 mL) broccoli florets
1 clove garlic, minced
1 ½-inch (1-cm) piece fresh ginger root, peeled
   and grated
¼ cup (50 mL) almonds, chopped
Salt to taste

❶ In bowl, moisten chicken in a mixture of corn-starch, water, soy sauce and sugar.

❷ Place wok or large frying pan over medium-high heat and pour in oil. When oil is sizzling, toss in broc-coli and stir-fry for 2 to 3 minutes or until tender-crisp. Remove from wok with a slotted spoon and set aside.

❸ Add chicken to wok and stir-fry for 2 to 3 minutes. Add garlic, ginger, broccoli and almonds.

Continue to stir and toss for 2 to 3 minutes or until mixture is heated through and chicken is still moist but no longer pink inside. Season with salt.

WHEN BUYING BROCCOLI, LOOK FOR TIGHTLY CLOSED,

DARK GREEN BUDS. YELLOW TIPS ARE A SIGN OF OLD AGE.

THE PEELED AND SHREDDED STALKS OF BROCCOLI MAKE A

GOOD ADDITION TO SALADS, STIR-FRIES AND SOUPS.

■ ■

Mexico

CHICKEN AND SPICES WRAPPED IN TORTILLAS

(Fajitas)

Serve this hot chili seasoned chicken fajita with a dollop of sour cream and a tossed green salad.

1 to 2 tbsp (15 to 25 mL) vegetable oil
1 boneless, skinless chicken breast or 2 thighs,
   cut into strips
1 small onion, chopped
½ green pepper, sliced
1 clove garlic, minced
1 tsp (5 mL) (or more) chopped jalapeño pepper
½ tsp (2 mL) each oregano and ground cumin, or
1 tsp (5 mL) commercial chili powder
¼ tsp (1 mL) salt
1 tomato, chopped
¼ cup (50 mL) whole black pitted olives
2 soft flour tortillas

❶ Place frying pan over medium-high heat and pour in oil. When oil is hot, add chicken and stir-fry for 1 to 2 minutes or until chicken is opaque. Reduce heat to medium-low and add onion, green pepper, garlic and jalapeño pepper. Stir and cook for 5 to 6 minutes or until vegetables are tender-crisp and chicken is no longer pink inside.

SERVES ONE

❷ Season with oregano, cumin and salt. Stir in tomato and olives and cook for another minute or until mixture is piping hot.

❸ Divide mixture between 2 tortillas and fold each tortilla in half.

IN CASE, LIKE ME, YOU ARE CONFUSED BY COOKING

TERMS: THE TORTILLA IS A FLAT BREAD MADE OF CORN

MEAL OR FLOUR; THE TACO IS A FRIED AND FILLED TORT-

ILLA; THE QUESADILLA IS A TORTILLA FILLED WITH CHEESE,

FOLDED AND DRY FRIED (WITHOUT OIL) AND THE ENCHI-

ADA IS A TORTILLA DIPPED IN SAUCE, FILLED AND BAKED.

SERVES TWO

United States

SOUTHERN FRIED CHICKEN AND GRAVY

Serve this Kentucky favorite with Perfect Mashed Potatoes (page 48) and a shredded sweet carrot and raisin salad.

½ chicken (about 1½ lb/750 g) cut into serving
  pieces
¼ cup (50 mL) all-purpose flour
¼ tsp (1 mL) each salt and granulated sugar
1 cup (250 mL) vegetable oil

GRAVY

1 tbsp (15 mL) all-purpose flour
¾ cup (175 mL) milk
¼ tsp (1 mL) each salt, pepper and nutmeg,
  or to taste

❶ Rinse and dry chicken pieces. Put flour, salt and sugar in paper bag. Drop chicken into bag and shake thoroughly to coat.

❷ Place cast-iron frying pan over high heat. Pour in oil to a depth of ¼ inch (5 mm). When oil is sizzling, add chicken pieces, skin side down, in a single layer. Cover pan, reduce heat to medium and pan-fry for 6 to 8 minutes or until golden brown. Turn over, cover pan and continue cooking for another 6 to 10 minutes or until chicken is tender and no longer pink inside. Remove breast before leg and thigh pieces because breasts cook faster. Place on plate in warm oven.

❸ *Gravy:* Pour off all but 1 tbsp (15 mL) of fat from pan. Over medium-low heat, stir in flour then whisk in milk. Continue stirring vigorously until gravy thickens. Season with salt, pepper and nutmeg, and simmer for 3 to 5 minutes. Spoon over chicken and mashed potatoes.

COLD LEFTOVER CHICKEN IS DELICIOUS IN RUSSIAN

POTATO, SAUSAGE AND CHICKEN SALAD (PAGE 35).

Japan
CHICKEN TERIYAKI
(Tori Teriyaki)

Teriyaki or "glaze broiled" is a favorite Japanese method of cooking. The sweet, pungent sauce is a useful marinade for meat, fish and tofu, as well as chicken. Serve Chicken Teriyaki with rice (page 54) and a sliced cucumber salad.

2 to 3 tbsp (25 to 45 mL) vegetable oil
1 chicken breast or leg with thigh attached

TERIYAKI SAUCE
¼ cup (50 mL) soy sauce
3 tbsp (45 mL) Japanese mirin or dry sherry
1 tbsp (15 mL) granulated sugar
1 clove garlic, minced
1 ½-inch (1-cm) piece fresh ginger root, peeled and grated
1 drop sesame oil (optional)

❶ *Teriyaki Sauce:* In shallow bowl or pie plate, combine soy sauce, mirin, sugar, garlic, ginger and sesame oil, if using. Add chicken and turn to coat both sides. Marinate for 1 hour if you have time. Drain and dry chicken, reserving the marinade.

❷ Place frying pan over medium heat and pour in oil. When oil is hot, add chicken skin side down. Pan-fry until golden brown, approximately 5 minutes per side. Pour sauce over chicken, cover pan, reduce heat to medium-low and cook for 10 minutes.

SERVES ONE

❸ Uncover and cook for 5 minutes more or until sauce has thickened and chicken is tender and no longer pink inside. Place chicken on warm plate and spoon sauce over top.

THERE ARE MANY COMMERCIAL VERSIONS OF TERIYAKI SAUCE. MAKING YOUR OWN IS SIMPLE, AND THE RESULTS ARE FRESHER AND LESS EXPENSIVE. IF YOU DOUBLE THE RECIPE, STORE THE REMAINDER IN THE REFRIGERATOR AND BE SURE TO USE IT WITHIN 3 OR 4 DAYS.

■■■■■■■■■■■■■■■■■■■■■■■■■■■■■

United States

CALIFORNIA LEMON CHICKEN

This slightly sweet, lemony chicken is refreshingly different. Serve with a green vegetable and pasta. For a change, try orzo, a tiny pasta that looks like rice and cooks very quickly.

1 or 2 chicken breasts or legs, thighs attached
¼ tsp (1 mL) each salt and ground ginger
1 tbsp (15 mL) all-purpose flour
2 tbsp (25 mL) vegetable oil
1 lemon, juice and grated rind (yellow skin only)
2 tbsp (25 mL) brown sugar
½ cup (125 mL) chicken stock or water

❶ Rinse and dry chicken. Sprinkle with salt, ginger and flour.

❷ Place ovenproof frying pan over medium heat and pour in oil. When oil is hot, add chicken pieces, skin side down, and pan-fry on both sides until brown and crisp, about 5 minutes per side.

❸ Sprinkle with lemon juice, rind and sugar. Pour stock around chicken. Finish cooking in 375°F (190°C) oven for 20 to 25 minutes. Alternatively, cover pan with a tight-fitting lid, reduce heat to simmer and cook for 15 minutes or until chicken is tender and no longer pink inside.

Bright yellow, thick-skinned lemons often have

very little juice. Choose thin-skinned ones and

warm them before squeezing for maximum juice.

Grated lemon rind can be frozen for later use.

SERVES ONE OR TWO

■ ■

India
CHICKEN CURRY WITH RAISINS
(Murgh Kari)

This spicy, aromatic dish is guaranteed to chase away the chicken blahs! Use commerical curry powder, or try my favorite curry spice mixture on page 160. Serve with Basic Long Grain Rice (page 56).

2 tbsp (25 mL) butter or vegetable oil
1 medium onion, chopped
2 cloves garlic, minced
1 tsp (5 mL) all-purpose flour
1 tsp (5 mL) curry powder (mild, medium or hot)
1 chicken leg with thigh attached or breast
½ cup (125 mL) chicken stock or water
1 tbsp (15 mL) raisins
¼ tsp (1 mL) salt
Pinch black pepper
Banana slices, plain yogurt

❶ In frying pan, melt butter over medium-low heat. Stir in onion and garlic and cook for 2 minutes or until onion is translucent. Sprinkle in flour and curry powder. Stir well. Add chicken and pan-fry, turning occasionally, for about 8 to 10 minutes, or until lightly brown on both sides.

❷ Stir in stock and raisins and bring to boil. Cover pan, reduce heat to low and simmer for 15 to 20 minutes or until chicken is tender and no longer pink inside. Remove chicken and place on warm plate.

❸ Thin sauce if necessary with a little stock or water, and add salt and pepper. To thicken, allow to boil rapidly for a few minutes. Pour sauce over chicken and garnish with banana and yogurt.

SERVES ONE

■■■■■■■■■■■■■■■■■■■■■■■■■■■■■■■■

Hungary

CHICKEN PAPRIKA

(Paprikás Csirke)

This sweet paprika-flavored chicken brings back vivid memories of my Hungarian ballet master. He adored this dish and cooked it in great lashings of butter. I have adapted his recipe, reducing the amount of fat in it. Serve with new nugget potatoes or noodles.

SERVES ONE

1 tbsp (15 mL) butter
1 tbsp (15 mL) vegetable oil
1 medium onion, chopped
1 tbsp (15 mL) paprika (preferably Hungarian)
1 skinless chicken breast or leg with thigh attached
½ green pepper, sliced
1 medium tomato, chopped
½ cup (125 mL) water
Sour cream (optional)

❶ In frying pan, melt butter and oil over medium-low heat. Add onion and cook for 2 minutes or until soft. Stir in paprika.

❷ Add chicken to pan and sauté for 5 to 6 minutes per side over medium heat. Stir in green pepper, tomato and water. Cover pan, reduce heat to low and simmer for 10 to 15 minutes or until chicken is tender and no longer pink inside.

❸ Remove chicken and vegetables with a slotted spoon and place on warm plate. Bring liquid in pan to boil and let bubble for 1 minute. Spoon over chicken and vegetables. Serve with a dollop of sour cream, if desired.

GREEN NOT RED OR YELLOW PEPPERS ARE THE MOST

REASONABLE IN PRICE AND HAPPILY THEY CONTAIN THE

HIGHEST LEVELS OF VITAMIN C.

■■■■■■■■■■■■■■■■■■■■■■■■■■■■■■■■

Ethiopia
CHICKEN BERBERE
(Doro Wat)

Chicken simmered in an amazing combination of a dozen herbs and spices called berbere is one of Ethiopia's most famous dishes. This simpler adaptation is served with sliced egg and flatbread (Injera) or pita bread.

SERVES ONE

Berbere

1 tsp (5 mL) ground ginger
3 tbsp (45 mL) cayenne pepper
¼ tsp (1 mL) ground cloves
½ tsp (2 mL) cinnamon
1 skinless chicken breast or leg with thigh
   attached
1 tbsp (15 mL) butter
1 tbsp (15 mL) vegetable oil
1 medium onion, chopped
2 cloves garlic, minced
1 tbsp (15 mL) tomato paste
½ cup (125 mL) water
Salt and pepper to taste
1 hard-cooked egg, sliced

❶ *Berbere:* Combine spices and store in an airtight jar.

❷ Rinse and pat dry chicken. With a sharp knife, score chicken in 2 or 3 places so that the sauce can penetrate.

❸ In cast-iron frying pan, melt butter and oil over medium heat. Add onion and garlic and sauté for 2 to 3 minutes or until onion is translucent. Sprinkle in ¼ tsp (1 mL) or more berbere (use caution, this is hot) and stir well. Add tomato paste and chicken and stir to coat chicken pieces. Stir in water, cover pan, and reduce heat to low. Simmer for 15 to 20 minutes or until chicken is tender and no longer pink inside. Stir and baste occasionally while cooking and add more water if it becomes dry. Season with salt and pepper.

❹ Place chicken and sauce on warm plate and garnish with sliced egg.

EVEN THE MOST DEPRESSING BITS OF MEAT AND TIRED

OLD VEGETABLES CAN BE GIVEN A BOOST WITH HERBS

AND SPICES. SAVE MONEY BY BUYING THEM IN SMALL

AMOUNTS IN BULK FOOD STORES.

■■■■■■■■■■■■■■■■■■■■■■■■■■■■■■■■■

Indonesia
CHICKEN WITH PEANUT SAUCE
(Saté Ayam)

This recipe is a quick and simple adaptation of an all-time favorite kebab of southeast Asia. If pushed for time, grill a boneless breast and use this rich and creamy peanut sauce for dipping. Serve with rice steamed with colorful bits of carrot, peas and grated lemon rind.

SERVES ONE

1 boneless, skinless chicken breast
1 tbsp (15 mL) soy sauce
1 tsp (5 mL) lemon juice
1 tsp (5 mL) oil (preferably sesame oil)

Peanut Sauce

½ cup (125 mL) boiling water
3 tbsp (45 mL) peanut butter
Juice of ½ lemon
¼ tsp (1 mL) each powdered garlic and salt
1 tbsp (15 mL) soy sauce
1 tsp (5 mL) brown or granulated sugar
Cayenne pepper or Tabasco sauce to taste
Coconut milk or water for thinning

❶ Slice chicken breast into strips about ½ inch (1 cm) wide and brush with soy sauce, lemon juice and oil. If desired, thread onto metal skewers or bamboo skewers that have been soaked in water.

❷ Place chicken on oiled broiler rack. Grill under preheated broiler about 2 inches (5 cm) from heat, about 3 to 4 minutes per side or until just cooked through. Do not overcook.

❸ *Peanut Sauce:* In small saucepan, combine water, peanut butter, lemon juice, garlic, salt, soy sauce, sugar and cayenne pepper. Mix well and bring mixture to boil. Reduce heat to low and simmer gently, uncovered, stirring until sauce thickens. If it is too thick, thin with coconut milk or water. Pour into a bowl and serve as a dipping sauce with the chicken strips.

UNSWEETENED COCONUT MILK CAN BE BOUGHT IN POW-

DERED FORM. MIXED WITH WATER, IT ADDS FLAVOR AND

RICHNESS TO SAUCES (SEE PAGE 62). DO NOT SUBSTITUTE

MILK FOR THE COCONUT MILK IN THIS RECIPE.

■ ■

Russia

CHICKEN PATTIES

(Kotleti)

These dill-scented patties from Soviet Georgia taste fantastic with cranberry sauce sharpened with cider vinegar, garlic and hot pepper. Apples and Potatoes (page 42) make an unusual accompaniment.

⅓ lb (150 g) ground chicken
½ cup (125 mL) dried breadcrumbs
½ small onion, grated
½ tsp (2 mL) crushed dill seed
Salt and pepper to taste
1 egg, beaten with a fork
2 tbsp (25 mL) vegetable oil
shredded lettuce garnish

❶ In a bowl, mix together chicken, 2 tbsp (25 mL) breadcrumbs, onion, dill, salt, pepper and half the beaten egg. Knead mixture with wet hands until well blended and shape into two patties.

❷ Dip patties into remaining egg and then into breadcrumbs.

❸ In frying pan heat oil. Brown patties over medium heat approximately 4 minutes on each side or until no longer pink inside. Place on a bed of shredded lettuce.

SERVES ONE

MEAT, NUTS AND TOFU

■■■■■■■■■■■■■■■■■■■■■■■■■■■■■■

Lebanon
SPICY BURGER IN PITA
(Dönor Kebab)

These moist and spicy meat patties are served inside pita bread or in a hamburger bun with a cucumber salad on the side.

⅓ lb (150 g) ground lamb or ground beef
2 tbsp (25 mL) dry bread crumbs
1 tbsp (15 mL) tomato sauce or ketchup
½ tsp (2 mL) (or more) ground cumin
Salt to taste
2 or 3 drops Tabasco sauce, or
Pinch cayenne pepper
1 tbsp (15 mL) vegetable oil
1 large round pita bread
1 tbsp (15 mL) Chick Pea Dip (page 34)
   (or commercial hummus)
1 small tomato, sliced
½ small onion, thinly sliced
4 tbsp (60 mL) plain yogurt
Shredded lettuce

❶ In bowl, mix together meat, bread crumbs, tomato sauce, cumin, salt and Tabasco sauce. Knead mixture with wet hands until well blended and shape into two 4-inch (10-cm) flat patties.

❷ Place frying pan over medium heat and pour in oil. When oil is hot, add patties and cook for 3 to 4 minutes per side for medium-rare. (Lower heat and cook longer for medium to well done.)

SERVES ONE

❸ Cut pita bread in half crosswise. Slit open to make a pocket and fill each half with meat patty, Chick-Pea Dip (if using), tomato and onion slices, and a dollop of yogurt. Place on a plate and garnish with shredded lettuce.

Always cook ground meats thoroughly.

Undercooked, rare hamburgers can cause a

severe illness, Hemolytic Uremic Syndrome or

"Hamburger Disease."

■■■■■■■■■■■■■■■■■■■■■■■■■■■■■■■

Malaysia

MEATBALLS IN SWEET-AND-SOUR SAUCE

(Daging lembu)

These slightly sweet, soy-seasoned balls with pineapple sauce make an interesting change served over rice. Try hot sugar peas as a side dish.

¹⁄₃ lb (150 g) ground beef
1 clove garlic, minced
1 tsp (5 mL) soy sauce
¹⁄₄ tsp (1 mL) each, salt, pepper and granulated
 sugar
¹⁄₄ cup (50 mL) all-purpose flour
1 tbsp (15 mL) vegetable oil

....

SWEET-AND-SOUR SAUCE

1 tsp (5 mL) cornstarch
³⁄₄ cup (175 mL) pineapple juice
1 tbsp (15 mL) soy sauce
1 tbsp (15 mL) white vinegar
1 ¹⁄₂-inch (1-cm) piece fresh ginger root, peeled
 and grated

❶ In medium bowl, mix together meat, garlic, soy sauce, salt, pepper and sugar. With wet hands, form into 5 walnut-sized balls. Roll in flour.

❷ In frying pan, heat oil. Pan-fry meatballs over medium heat for 5 to 6 minutes, shaking pan and turning with tongs until brown all over. Drain off excess fat.

SERVES ONE

❸ *Sweet-and-Sour Sauce:* In small saucepan, combine all sauce ingredients. Stir well to dissolve cornstarch in cold liquid.

❹ Place saucepan over medium heat and cook mixture, stirring constantly, for 1 to 2 minutes or until clear and slightly thickened. Pour sauce over meatballs and simmer for 30 seconds or just until heated through. Serve meatballs on a mound of hot rice and pour sauce over all.

MIX UP A DOUBLE BATCH OF MEATBALLS AND FREEZE

THEM ON A BAKING SHEET. WHEN FROZEN, PLACE

INDIVIDUAL SERVINGS IN PLASTIC BAGS AND PUT IN

THE FREEZER.

Italy
LEMON PARMESAN MEATBALLS
(Palline di Carne)

SERVES TWO

A hint of lemon makes these meatballs deliziose. Serve over spaghetti and sprinkle with grated Parmesan cheese. If cooking for one, leftovers will make a great meatball sandwich.

1 egg, beaten with a fork
1 to 2 tbsp (15 to 25 mL) grated Parmesan cheese
1 clove garlic, minced
¼ cup (50 mL) dry bread crumbs
Juice of ½ lemon
¼ tsp (1 mL) each salt and pepper
½ tsp (2 mL) each basil and oregano
½ lb (250 g) ground beef
2 to 3 tbsp (25 to 45 mL) canola or olive oil
½ cup (125 mL) Tomato Sauce (page 146) or
   canned tomato sauce

❶ In large bowl, mix together egg, cheese, garlic, bread crumbs, lemon juice and seasonings. Add meat, knead mixture with wet hands until well combined and form into walnut-sized balls.

❷ In frying pan, heat oil. Pan-fry meatballs over medium heat for 5 to 6 minutes or until brown. Shake pan and turn balls with tongs or a spoon to keep from sticking. Pour in tomato sauce, immediately cover with a lid and reduce heat to low.

❸ Cook gently for another 5 minutes, stirring meatballs from time to time to coat with sauce. Add a little boiling water if there isn't enough sauce in bottom of pan.

■■■■■■■■■■■■■■■■■■■■■■■■■■■■■■■

Sweden
SWEDISH MEATBALLS
(Små Köttbullar)

*Serve these creamy, nutmeg-scented meatballs in a nest of
Perfect Mashed Potatoes (page 48).*

⅓ cup (75 mL) dry bread crumbs
½ small onion, grated
1 egg, beaten with a fork
¼ tsp (1 mL) each salt and pepper
¼ tsp (1 mL) each nutmeg and allspice
⅓ lb (150 g) ground beef
2 tbsp (25 mL) vegetable oil
4 tbsp (60 mL) whipping or light cream

❶ In large bowl, mix together bread crumbs, onion,
beaten egg and seasonings. Add meat, knead mixture
with wet hands until well combined and form into
walnut-sized balls.

❷ In frying pan, heat oil. Brown meatballs over
medium heat for 6 to 8 minutes. Shake pan and turn
with tongs or a spoon to keep from sticking.

❸ Spoon off any excess fat from frying pan. Reduce
heat to low. Pour in cream and spoon over meatballs.
Cover with a lid and simmer gently for 8 to 10 minutes or until cream thickens slightly. Do not allow
cream to boil.

SERVES ONE

■■■■■■■■■■■■■■■■■■■■■■■■■■■■■■

Morocco

SWEET AND SPICY MEATBALLS

(Kefta Tagine)

SERVES ONE

These fast and easy meatballs capture all the pungent smells of an exotic North African tagine. Serve them with rice or Couscous (page 154) to soak up the delicious fruity sauce.

⅓ lb (150 g) ground lamb or beef
½ small onion, grated
¼ tsp (1 mL) each ground cumin and cinnamon
1 or 2 drops Tabasco sauce, or
Pinch cayenne pepper
2 to 3 tbsp (25 to 45 mL) vegetable oil

....

SAUCE

1 tbsp (15 mL) vegetable oil (preferably olive oil)
½ onion, chopped
1 clove garlic, minced
½ green pepper, chopped
1 tbsp (15 mL) tomato paste mixed with
   ¾ cup (175 mL) water
2 to 3 tbsp (25 to 45 mL) raisins, dates or prunes,
   chopped
1 tsp (5 mL) brown sugar
¼ tsp (1 mL) ground cloves or nutmeg
¼ tsp (1 mL) cinnamon
Salt and pepper to taste

❶ In large bowl, mix together meat, onion and seasonings. With wet hands, form into walnut-sized balls.

❷ In frying pan, heat oil. Pan-fry meatballs over medium heat for 6 minutes or until brown. Shake pan and turn with tongs or a spoon to keep from sticking.

❸ *Sauce:* In saucepan, heat oil. Add onion and garlic and cook over medium-low heat for 1 to 2 minutes or until onion is translucent. Stir in green pepper, tomato sauce, raisins, brown sugar and seasonings. Bring to boil. Immediately remove from heat.

❹ Pour sauce over meatballs. Reduce heat to low, cover and simmer for about 10 minutes, stirring occasionally until mixture has thickened slightly and meatballs are cooked through.

TO SOFTEN ROCK-HARD BROWN SUGAR, SIMPLY ADD A SLICE OF SOFT BREAD TO THE PACKAGE AND SEAL TIGHTLY. IN A FEW HOURS THE SUGAR WILL BE SOFT AGAIN. ALTERNATELY, IF NEEDED IMMEDIATELY, GRATE THE SUGAR.

SERVES TWO

■■■■■■■■■■■■■■■■■■■■■■■■■■■■■■■■

Canada
HERBED NO-MEAT BALLS
(Petites Boulettes)

This recipe makes vegetarian mock meatballs that taste surprisingly like the real thing. Serve them with tomato sauce over piping hot linguine and sprinkle with grated Parmesan cheese.

½ lb (250 g) tofu, drained
¾ cup (175 mL) rolled oats
1 small onion, finely minced
1 egg, beaten with a fork
2 tbsp (25 mL) Japanese soy sauce
1 tbsp (15 mL) Dijon mustard
1 tsp (5 mL) apple cider vinegar
¼ tsp (1 mL) each basil and oregano
Pinch pepper, or to taste
3 tbsp (45 mL) vegetable oil
¾ cup (175 mL) Tomato Sauce (page 146)
1 tsp (5 mL) chopped fresh basil (optional)

❶ In large bowl, crumble tofu and add rolled oats, onion, egg, soy sauce, mustard, vinegar and seasonings. With wet hands, knead mixture and shape into walnut-sized balls.

❷ In frying pan, heat oil. Add balls and pan-fry over medium-low heat for 4 to 5 minutes or until brown and heated through. Shake pan to keep from sticking.

❸ Pour Tomato Sauce over balls and simmer gently, uncovered, for another 3 minutes. Serve on warm plate over pasta.

■ ■

Turkey
GRILLED MEATBALLS
(Cizbiz Köfte)

These finger- or sausage-shaped meat patties are boldly spiced with the flavors of Istanbul. Serve with Spicy Golden Pilaf (page 70) and unflavored yogurt.

SERVES ONE

1 tbsp (15 mL) olive or vegetable oil
½ small onion, grated
3 tbsp (45 mL) fresh bread crumbs
1 clove garlic, minced
½ tsp (2 ml) each ground cumin and dried mint
¼ tsp (1 mL) each salt and nutmeg
Pinch black pepper
⅓ lb (150 g) ground lamb or beef
Tomato wedges

❶ Preheat oven broiler and lightly oil broiler rack.

❷ In large bowl, mix together onion, bread crumbs, garlic and seasonings. Add meat, knead mixture with wet hands until well combined, and shape into 1-inch (2.5-cm) thick sausages.

❸ Place on broiler pan and grill 2 to 3 inches (5 to 8 cm) from heat for 5 to 6 minutes per side. Garnish with tomato wedges.

Variation: Split a small baguette or hot dog bun in half and fill with spicy meat patties and your choice of onions, tomato slices and crunchy green pepper.

■ ■

Canada
NUT BURGER DELUXE
(Galette aux herbes)

This moist and crunchy vegetarian burger is rich in protein. Parmesan Potato Wedges (page 50) make a great accompaniment.

½ cup (125 mL) ground walnuts
½ cup (125 mL) dry bread crumbs
1 small onion, grated
1 clove garlic, minced
1 egg, beaten with a fork
1 tsp (5 mL) mayonnaise
1 tsp (5 mL) soy sauce
Pinch black pepper
1 tbsp (15 mL) butter
1 large hamburger bun
Sliced tomatoes, cucumbers, pickles, relish,
    ketchup, mustard

❶ In large bowl, mix together walnuts, bread crumbs, onion, garlic, egg, mayonnaise, soy sauce and seasonings. With wet hands, squeeze and pat mixture together to make a flat patty.

❷ In frying pan, melt butter over medium-low heat. Cook patty for about 5 minutes per side.

❸ Split, toast and butter bun. Arrange all your favorite hamburger condiments on bun and top with patty.

SERVES ONE

■ ■

Mexico
BEEF TACOS WITH SPICY SAUCE
(Tacos Con Carne y Salsa Picante)

*Serve these popular cumin-spiced tacos with shredded lettuce,
a favorite cheese, lettuce, olives and a squeeze of lemon.*

S E R V E S   O N E

⅓ cup (75 mL) vegetable oil
2 corn tortillas or ready-to-fill taco shells
1 small onion, chopped
1 clove garlic, minced
¼ lb (125 g) ground beef
½ tsp (2 mL) each ground cumin and oregano
¼ tsp (1 mL) salt
Pinch cayenne pepper
1 to 2 tbsp (15 to 25 mL) Mexican salsa (page 8)

❶ In frying pan, heat oil over high heat and fry tortillas, one at a time, for 10 seconds. Fold in half and fry on each side until crisp (about 30 seconds total). Place in oven to keep warm.

❷ Pour off all but 1 tbsp (15 mL) of oil. Place pan over medium-low heat. Add onion and garlic and cook for 2 minutes or until onion is translucent. Add meat and brown, stirring occasionally, for 7 to 8 minutes. Add seasonings and salsa. Reduce heat to low and simmer gently for another 3 minutes.

❸ Fill warmed tortillas with meat mixture and garnish with your choice of toppings.

Variation: To make vegetarian tacos, substitute cooked and mashed pinto beans for the ground beef.

■■■■■■■■■■■■■■■■■■■■■■■■■■■■■■■

Italy
ITALIAN MEAT SAUCE
(Ragù)

Italian meat sauce has probably kept more single people from starvation than any other recipe. This classic sauce is terrific over any type of pasta — spaghetti, linguine, macaroni — but also try it over baked potatoes and on crusty warm buns, split and buttered. Freeze leftover sauce in single-sized portions in plastic freezer bags.

¼ cup (50 mL) vegetable oil
2 tbsp (25 mL) olive oil
1 large onion, chopped
2 cloves garlic, minced
2 lb (1 kg) ground beef
2 large carrots, scrubbed and grated
2 or 3 stalks celery, chopped
1 can (5½ oz/156 mL) tomato paste
1 cup (250 mL) water
1 can (28 oz/796 mL) plum tomatoes and juice
1 tbsp (15 mL) each oregano and basil
½ tsp (2 mL) each salt, pepper and granulated
  sugar
½ tsp (2 mL) nutmeg
¼ tsp (1 mL) crushed bay leaf

❶ In large frying pan or heavy-bottomed saucepan, heat vegetable and olive oils. Cook onion and garlic over medium-low heat for 1 to 2 minutes or until onion is translucent. Add meat, carrots and celery.

MAKES 8 CUPS (2 L)

Cook, stirring and breaking up lumps, for 6 to 8 minutes until meat is light brown.

❷ Stir in tomato paste, water, tomatoes, juice, and seasonings. Bring to boil, then reduce heat to low. Allow to simmer, uncovered, for at least 45 minutes, stirring from time to time.

Variation: For a meatless savory sauce, substitute any cooked white bean (navy, white kidney, cannellini) or firm tofu for meat.

Mexico

MEXICAN MEAT SAUCE

(Picadillo)

SERVES TWO

Ladle this hot and spicy sauce over baked potatoes, pinto beans, or into a Rice Pie Crust (page 59). For a cool contrast, serve with sour cream.

2 to 3 tbsp (25 to 45 mL) vegetable oil
1 medium onion, chopped
2 cloves garlic, minced
½ lb (250 g) ground beef
½ tsp (2 mL) chili powder
½ tsp (2 mL) each ground cumin, oregano and
   granulated sugar
¼ tsp (1 mL) each salt and pepper
Red pepper flakes or cayenne pepper to taste
½ can (14 oz/398 mL) crushed tomatoes
   and juice

❶ In frying pan, heat oil. Cook onion over medium heat for 3 minutes or until soft. Add garlic, meat and seasonings, and stir well.

❷ When meat is browned, add tomato and juice and cook for 4 to 5 minutes.

❸ Taste and adjust seasoning, if necessary. Reduce heat to low and simmer gently, adding a little boiling water if it becomes dry, 15 minutes or more, stirring from time to time.

LEFTOVERS CAN BE ROLLED UP IN SOFT TORTILLAS TOPPED

WITH CHEESE AND BAKED UNTIL HEATED THROUGH.

■ ■

Bavaria
SAUSAGES IN BEER SAUCE
(Bratwurst mit Bier)

This is an old and delicious recipe that makes sausages special. Serve with egg noodles or fettuccine.

3 or 4 fresh bratwurst or pork sausages
4 tbsp (60 mL) all-purpose flour
3 tbsp (45 mL) butter or vegetable oil
1 large onion, sliced
¾ cup (175 mL) beer
1 tbsp (15 mL) tomato paste
Salt and pepper to taste

SERVES ONE

❶ Bring pot of water to boil. Remove from heat, add sausages and soak for 5 minutes. Drain sausages and roll in flour.

❷ In frying pan, melt butter over medium heat. Brown sausages, turning until crispy, 2 to 3 minutes. Remove from pan and place on paper towel. Add onion to pan. Stir and cook for 2 minutes or until onion is translucent. Return sausages to pan.

❸ In small bowl, mix together beer and tomato paste. Pour over sausages and onion, reduce heat to low, cover and simmer for 5 to 6 minutes or until sauce thickens and flavors meld. Add salt and pepper.

WITH A BEER KIT OF HOP-FLAVORED MALT AND BREWER'S YEAST PLUS SUGAR AND WATER, 5 GALLONS (18 L) OF UNFORGETTABLE LAGER CAN BE PRODUCED AND READY TO DRINK WITHIN TWO WEEKS.

■■■■■■■■■■■■■■■■■■■■■■■■■■■■■■

Singapore
BEEF AND ORANGE STIR-FRY
(Ngau Yook)

A tiny steak goes a long way when sliced paper thin and served with gingery orange slices and Chinese egg noodles.

4 tbsp (60 mL) light soy sauce
2 tsp (10 mL) granulated sugar
1 tsp (5 mL) cornstarch
½ cup (125 mL) Basic Meat Stock (page 26)
   or water
Pinch black pepper
1 ½-inch (1-cm) piece fresh ginger root, peeled
   and shredded
2 bundles dried oriental egg noodles
2 to 3 tbsp (25 to 45 mL) vegetable oil (canola)
1 clove garlic, crushed
¼ lb (125 g) beef steak, sliced paper thin at
   an angle
1 medium onion, sliced
1 stalk celery, sliced on an angle
1 or 2 oranges, peeled and sliced
Sesame seeds (optional)

❶ In cup, mix together soy sauce, sugar, cornstarch, cold stock, pepper and ginger. Stir well to remove lumps.

❷ Place egg noodle bundles in saucepan of cold water, bring to boil and cook until just tender, about 1 minute.

❸ In wok or frying pan, heat oil over high heat. When oil is sizzling, toss in garlic for 30 seconds to perfume oil. Remove with a slotted spoon and discard. Immediately add beef and stir-fry for 1 minute. Push to one side and add onion and celery, or other vegetables of your choice. Cook for another 30 seconds. Add oranges and cook just until heated through. Push all ingredients to one side. Pour soy sauce mixture in center of wok and stir until sauce becomes translucent, about 30 seconds. Mix all ingredients together, coating beef and orange with sauce. Pour over hot, drained egg noodles and sprinkle with sesame seeds, if desired.

TOUGH MEAT IS MORE TENDER WHEN THINLY SLICED

AND IT IS EASIER TO SLICE IF VERY COLD. A MARINADE

WITH EQUAL PARTS OIL AND VINEGAR ALSO HELPS TO

TENDERIZE MEAT.

■ ■

Hungary

SMOKED SAUSAGE WITH PAPRIKA SAUCE

(Lescó)

There are two kinds of sausages: fresh sausages, which must be thoroughly cooked before eating, and cured sausages, which only need to be heated through. This recipe is for smoke-cured sausage and is delicious served with Basic Long Grain Rice (page 56) or potatoes.

1 to 2 tbsp (15 to 25 mL) vegetable oil
1 medium onion, chopped
1 tbsp (15 mL) paprika (preferably Hungarian)
¼ tsp (1 mL) salt
1 medium tomato, chopped
1 green pepper, sliced
1 tsp (5 mL) granulated sugar
¼ lb (125 g) smoked sausage, sliced

❶ In frying pan, heat oil. Add onion, paprika and salt and cook over medium heat, stirring constantly, for 1 to 2 minutes or until onion is translucent.

❷ Add tomato, green pepper and sugar. Stir well and add sausage. Cover pan, reduce heat to medium-low and simmer for 10 to 15 minutes or until sauce thickens slightly and flavors meld.

❸ Place sausage on warm plate and pour sauce on top.

SERVES ONE

■■■■■■■■■■■■■■■■■■■■■■■■■■■■■ ■■

China

TOFU WITH GARLIC HONEY SAUCE

(Dau Fu)

Tofu absorbs the subtle honey-soy sauce in this simple recipe that goes well with Oriental Short Grain Rice (page 54) and a lettuce and bean sprout salad.

SERVES ONE

....

SAUCE

1 clove garlic, minced

¼ tsp (1 mL) salt

1 ½-inch (1-cm) piece fresh ginger root, peeled and shredded

1 tbsp (15 mL) lightly salted soy sauce

1 tbsp (15 mL) honey or granulated sugar

1 tbsp (15 mL) dry sherry or fruit juice

¼ cup (50 mL) vegetable stock or water

¼ tsp (1 mL) five spice powder <u>OR</u>

¼ tsp (1 mL) each cinnamon and ground cloves

1 tbsp (15 mL) vegetable oil

8 oz (250 g) fresh, firm tofu

Chopped green onions

❶ In bowl, mix together sauce ingredients. Stir well.

❷ In frying pan, heat oil over medium heat. Gently sauté 1-inch (2.5-cm) thick slices of tofu for 1 to 2 minutes or until heated through and lightly brown. Add sauce to pan and simmer, uncovered, for 3 to 4 minutes or until sauce thickens slightly.

❸ With a spatula, place tofu on plate and spoon sauce over top. Garnish with chopped green onions.

United States

POLENTA WITH WALNUTS, GARLIC AND PEARS

Called mamaliga in Soviet Georgia, ugali in Kenya, polenta in Italy, this is a classic cornmeal dish that has enjoyed renewed popularity. It is simple to make and complements your favorite fruit, nuts and cheeses.

1½ cups (375 mL) water
¼ tsp (1 mL) salt
½ cup (125 mL) quick cooking cornmeal
4 tbsp (60 mL) vegetable oil
4 tbsp (60 mL) walnut pieces
2 cloves garlic, minced
1 small pear, diced
2 tbsp (30 mL) blue cheese (optional)

❶ In a saucepan, bring water to a boil. Add salt and slowly sprinkle in cornmeal stirring vigorously with wooden spoon. Turn heat to medium low and stir constantly 4 to 5 minutes, until mixture is very thick.

❷ Turn mixture onto a pie plate, press flat like a patty, allow to cool slightly, and cut into rough squares.

❸ In a small bowl, combine and crush with a wooden spoon oil, walnuts and garlic. Pour mixture over the cornmeal squares and toss lightly.

❹ Sprinkle with pears and crumbled cheese if desired, and bake in a 375° F (190° C) oven for 10 minutes, until piping hot.

SERVES ONE

PASTA

■ ■

Italy

PASTA WITH OLIVE OIL, GARLIC AND HOT CHILI PEPPER

(Spaghetti con Aglio, Olio e Peperoncino)

This fiery hot classic pasta dish is for unashamed garlic lovers. Adjust the amount of red chili to taste. A crisp and crunchy cheese, nut and celery salad makes a fine accompaniment.

4 to 6 oz (125 to 170 g) dried spaghetti
¼ cup (50 mL) olive oil
2 or 3 cloves garlic, chopped
1 small fresh red chili pepper, chopped, or
3 or 4 drops chili oil
Salt and pepper to taste
Parmesan cheese

❶ In large pot, bring water to boil. Add salt, if desired. Add spaghetti and stir until water returns to boil. Cook, uncovered, stirring occasionally, for 8 to 10 minutes or until *al dente* (tender but not soft).

❷ In frying pan, heat olive oil over medium heat. Add garlic and chili pepper and cook for 20 seconds or just until garlic releases its fragrance. Do not allow to brown; overcooked garlic turns bitter.

❸ Drain spaghetti and immediately toss with garlic olive oil, salt and pepper. Pile onto warm plate and sprinkle with Parmesan cheese.

FOR ONE GENEROUS SERVING OF PASTA, TAKE A HANDFUL

OF DRIED SPAGHETTI, A LITTLE LESS THAN THE DIAMETER

OF A GARDEN HOSE.

SERVES ONE

■■■■■■■■■■■■■■■■■■■■■■■■■■■■■■■■■

Thailand
SPICY THAI NOODLES
(Mah Mee)

Two bundles of dried Chinese egg noodles makes 1½ cups (375 mL) of cooked noodles. Thai rice noodles (rice sticks) or Italian vermicelli (broken in half) may be substituted. See instructions on package for cooking.

2 bundles dried Chinese egg noodles
2 to 3 tbsp (25 to 45 mL) peanut butter
1 clove garlic, minced
2 tbsp (30 mL) Thai fish sauce
1 tbsp (15 mL) lemon juice
1 tsp (5 mL) sesame oil
2 or 3 drops hot chili oil or Tabasco sauce
½ tsp (2 mL) granulated sugar
2 cups (500 mL) favorite raw vegetables,
  slivered, sliced or grated
Peanuts (optional)

❶ In saucepan of boiling water, cook noodles for 3 to 4 minutes. Drain and place in warm bowl.

❷ In small pot, stir together peanut butter, garlic, fish sauce, lemon juice, sesame oil, hot chili oil and sugar over low heat until smooth and warm, about 1 minute. If necessary, thin with 1 or 2 spoonfuls of hot water.

❸ Put vegetables in colander and rinse in very hot water (or steam for 2 or 3 minutes if you prefer). Toss noodles and veggies together and dress with the peanut mixture. For added crunch and protein, garnish with peanuts.

SERVES ONE

■■■■■■■■■■■■■■■■■■■■■■■■■■■■■■

Italy

PASTA WITH BASIL AND PINE NUTS

(Pesto alla Genovese)

For those who do not possess a food processor, here is a fresh and crunchy variation of a classic pesto sauce.

SERVES ONE

½ cup (125 mL) fresh basil (about 15 leaves)
3 tbsp (45 mL) (or more) pine nuts, roughly chopped
2 or 3 cloves garlic, minced
4 tbsp (60 mL) grated Parmesan cheese
½ cup (125 ml) olive oil or a mixture of less expensive canola oil and olive oil
Salt and pepper to taste
⅓ lb (150 g) dried linguine or spaghetti
Pine nuts, sliced tomato

❶ On cutting board, slice basil into fine strips and bruise with the flat of the knife.

❷ In bowl, combine basil, pine nuts, garlic and Parmesan cheese. Stir in oil and season with salt and pepper. For the best flavor, allow mixture to stand at room temperature for 1 hour.

❸ Bring a large pot of water to boil, add ½ tsp (2 mL) salt if desired, and stir until water returns to boil. Cook uncovered, stirring occasionally, for 8 to 10 minutes or until *al dente* (tender but not soft). Drain briefly, return to pot and stir in basil and oil mixture. Toss with two forks and pile onto warm plate. Garnish with extra pine nuts and serve with a sliced tomato.

■■■■■■■■■■■■■■■■■■■■■■■■■■■■■■■

Italy

FETTUCCINE WITH CREAM AND PARMESAN

(Fettuccine all' Alfredo)

This is a special treat when you crave something rich and creamy. It beats me why anyone would buy an expensive pack-aged Alfredo sauce mix when it is so easy and quick to make. Serve with a fresh, crisp salad dressed with lemon juice.

⅓ lb (150 g) dried fettuccine or spaghetti
⅓ cup (75 mL) whipping cream
4 tbsp (60 mL) (or more) grated Parmesan cheese
1 tbsp (15 mL) butter
Black pepper, Parmesan cheese

❶ In large pot, bring water to boil. Add salt, if desired. Add pasta and stir until water returns to boil. Cook uncovered, stirring occasionally, for 8 to 10 minutes or until *al dente* (tender but not soft). Fresh pasta will cook in less time but costs a lot more.

❷ Drain and immediately return to pot. Pour in cream, sprinkle Parmesan cheese on top and add butter. Toss with two forks and pile onto warm plate.

❸ Sprinkle pepper on top and extra Parmesan cheese.

HOLLYWOOD STARS DOUGLAS FAIRBANKS, JR. AND

MARY PICKFORD ENJOYED THIS PASTA SO MUCH THAT

THEY PRESENTED A PAIR OF 18 KARAT GOLD FORKS TO

ALFREDO IN HIS RESTAURANT IN ROME.

SERVES ONE

■ ■

Greece

PASTA WITH BEANS AND GREENS

(Makarónia mè Spanaki)

Don't let these simple ingredients fool you — the combination of flavors is complex and very satisfying. Serve with a green salad sprinkled with a little crumbled feta cheese and olives.

3 tbsp (45 mL) canola or olive oil
1 clove garlic, minced
1 small onion, sliced
3 or 4 large leaves of spinach or Swiss chard
½ to ¾ cup (125 to 175 mL) cooked chick-peas
1 medium tomato, chopped
½ lemon, juice and grated rind (yellow skin only)
Chopped fresh parsley
3 or 4 fresh mint leaves (optional)
Salt and pepper to taste
⅓ lb (150 g) dried spaghetti
1 tsp (5 mL) salt (optional)

❶ In frying pan, heat oil. Add garlic and onion and sauté over medium-low heat for 1 minute.

❷ Add shredded spinach to pan. Cook until wilted then stir in chick-peas, tomato, lemon juice and rind, parsley, mint (if using), salt and pepper. Cook for 4 to 5 minutes.

❸ In large pot, bring water to boil. Add salt, if desired. Add spaghetti and stir until water returns to boil. Cook uncovered, stirring occasionally, for 8 to 10 minutes or until *al dente* (tender but not soft).

❹ Drain, return to pot and add spinach and chick-pea mixture. Toss with two forks and pile onto warm plate.

Peas, beans or seeds? The words seem to be interchangeable. A chick-pea is the same thing as a garbanzo bean or ceci; the black-eyed pea is a cow pea as well as a black-eyed bean; and the pigeon pea is a Congo bean. However, they are all the edible seeds of a pod-bearing plant.

■■■■■■■■■■■■■■■■■■■■■■■■■■■■■■

Israel

PASTA WITH COTTAGE CHEESE AND RAISINS

(Lochshen Kaesekugel)

Like many Israeli dishes, this one is a little sweet, a little sour and very rich for special occasions. It is possible, of course, to reduce the calorie-cholesterol count with low-fat substitutes without reducing the creamy texture. Serve with pita bread and a crisp green salad sprinkled with chick-peas and lemon juice.

⅓ lb (150 g) dried broad egg noodles
1 tbsp (15 mL) butter
½ cup (125 mL) cottage cheese, dry or lightly
  creamed
½ cup (125 mL) sour cream
1 tbsp (15 mL) raisins or currants
1 tsp (5 mL) granulated sugar
Salt to taste

❶ In saucepan, bring water to boil. Add salt, if desired. Add egg noodles and stir until water returns to boil. Cook uncovered, stirring occasionally, according to package instructions. (Egg noodles cook faster than durum wheat pasta.) Drain and return to pot placed over low heat.

❷ Add butter, cottage cheese, sour cream, raisins and sugar to hot noodles. Stir to combine. Add salt to taste.

❸ Pile onto warm plate.

SERVES ONE OR TWO

■ ■

United States
SPINACH FETTUCCINE WITH VEGETABLES AND HAM

A pale green pasta with multi-colored vegetables looks as good as it tastes. You can, and are encouraged to, choose seasonal vegetables to suit your budget.

SERVES ONE

⅓ lb (150 g) dried spinach fettuccine
1 small carrot, peeled and cut into matchsticks
1 broccoli stalk, peeled and cut into matchsticks
3 or 4 green beans, sliced lengthwise
1 tbsp (15 mL) butter
2 cloves garlic, minced
2 or 3 mushrooms, sliced
4 oz (125 g) cooked ham, chicken or tofu, cubed
4 tbsp (60 mL) whipping cream
2 tbsp (25 mL) Parmesan cheese
Salt and pepper to taste

❶ In large pot, bring water to boil. Add salt if desired. Add fettuccine and stir until water returns to boil. Cook uncovered, stirring occasionally, for 5 minutes. Add vegetables slowly so that water continues to boil and cook another 2 to 3 minutes or until pasta is *al dente* (tender but not soft) and vegetables are heated through.

❷ Meanwhile, in frying pan, melt butter over medium-low heat. Stir in garlic, mushrooms and ham. Simmer gently for 1 minute.

❸ Drain pasta and vegetables and return to pan in which they were cooked. Add mushroom mixture, cream and Parmesan cheese, and season with salt and pepper. Toss with two forks and serve on warm plate.

■■■■■■■■■■■■■■■■■■■■■■■■■■■■

France

PASTA WITH ZUCCHINI

(Pâtes aux Courgettes)

SERVES ONE

This recipe from southwest France is very useful in midsummer when zucchini are so prolific. If you have only enormous zucchini, chop into large bite-sized chunks; otherwise, slice small ones in rounds. Serve this dish with crisp bacon and a salad or with grilled chicken.

2 cups (500 mL) sliced or chopped zucchini
3 tbsp (45 mL) vegetable oil, preferably olive oil
1 clove garlic, minced
3 or 4 fresh basil leaves, finely sliced, or
½ tsp (2 mL) dried basil
Salt and pepper to taste
⅓ lb (150 g) dried spaghetti
¾ cup (125 mL) grated farmer's or Gruyère cheese

❶ Place frying pan over medium heat and pour in oil. Sauté zucchini for 2 to 3 minutes. Season with garlic, basil, salt and pepper. Cover pan and cook for another 5 minutes, stirring occasionally.

❷ In large pot, bring water to boil. Add salt, if desired. Add pasta and stir until water returns to boil. Cook uncovered, stirring occasionally, for 6 to 8 minutes or until *al dente* (tender but not soft). Drain and return to pot. Toss in zucchini mixture and mix well.

❸ Pile onto warm plate and top with grated cheese.

■ ■

Italy

MACARONI WITH FRESH RIPE TOMATOES

(Pomodori alla maggiorana)

This Sardinian dish is perfect for late summer when tomatoes are abundant. Serve with warm crusty rolls and a chopped celery and chick-pea salad.

SERVES ONE

2 large tomatoes, diced
1 cup (250 mL) diced mozzarella or farmer's cheese
2 cloves garlic, minced
4 tbsp (60 mL) olive or canola oil
½ tsp (2 mL) dried marjoram or 1 sprig, fresh
Salt and pepper to taste
1½ cups (375 mL) dried macaroni or shell pasta
Chopped green onions

❶ In medium bowl, combine tomatoes, cheese, garlic, oil, marjoram, salt and pepper. Let stand at room temperature.

❷ In pot, bring water to boil. Add salt, if desired. Add macaroni and stir until water returns to boil. Cook uncovered, stirring occasionally, for 6 to 7 minutes or until tender.

❸ Drain and immediately stir in tomato and cheese mixture. Pile into warm bowl and garnish with green onions.

Freeze tomatoes in plastic freezer bags. When thawed, tomatoes lose their shape, but not their flavor, and are perfect for sauces.

■ ■

Italy

SPAGHETTI WITH TOMATO SAUCE

(Sugo di Pomodoro)

Quite simply, a perfect spaghetti sauce, pizza sauce, topping for garlic toast (bruschetta) and sauce for Rice Cakes with Mozzarella (page 68).

Tomato Sauce

4 tbsp (60 mL) canola or olive oil

1 large onion, sliced

2 cloves garlic, minced

½ tsp (2 mL) each basil and oregano

¼ tsp (1 mL) (or more) nutmeg

1 tbsp (15 mL) each granulated sugar and apple cider vinegar

Salt and pepper to taste

1 can (28 oz/796 mL) plum or crushed tomatoes and juice

⅓ lb (150 g) dried spaghetti

Oil or butter (optional)

3 or 4 tbsp (45 to 60 mL) grated Parmesan cheese

❶ *Tomato Sauce:* In large frying pan or heavy-bottomed saucepan, heat oil over medium-low heat. Add onion and cook for 5 minutes. Add garlic, basil, oregano, nutmeg, sugar, vinegar, salt, pepper and tomatoes. Crush tomatoes with a spoon and stir well. Cover and simmer gently, stirring occasionally, for at least 15 minutes, preferably 30 minutes or more.

MAKES 3 CUPS (750 mL)

❷ In large pot of boiling, salted water, cook spaghetti for 8 to 10 minutes or until *al dente* (tender but not soft). Drain and return to pot. Toss with a spoonful of oil or butter, if desired.

❸ Pile spaghetti on warm plate and top with tomato sauce, ½ cup (125 mL) or more according to appetite, and sprinkle with Parmesan cheese.

MAKING YOUR OWN TOMATO SAUCE COSTS HALF AS

MUCH AS READY-TO-SERVE AND TASTES 100 TIMES

BETTER. USE CHOPPED FRESH TOMATOES WHEN IN

SEASON. THIS SAUCE CAN BE FROZEN IN REUSABLE

PLASTIC FREEZER BAGS IN SERVING-SIZED PORTIONS.

■ ■

Italy

PASTA WITH CLAM AND TOMATO SAUCE

(Vermicelli con le Vongole)

Of the many recipes for clam sauce, this Neapolitan version is the one that I prefer. The slight sweetness of the tomato with the baby clams is a perfect combination. This dish uses only half a can of clams; the rest can be used to make a delicious clam chowder (page 29).

1 to 2 tbsp (15 to 25 mL) canola or olive oil
1 medium onion, chopped
1 clove garlic, minced
1 tbsp (15 mL) tomato paste
½ cup (125 mL) water
1 medium tomato, chopped
1 tsp (5 mL) granulated sugar
½ tsp (2 mL) each basil and oregano
Salt and pepper to taste
½ can (10 oz/284 g) baby clams, undrained
⅓ lb (150 g) dried vermicelli or spaghetti
1 tbsp (15 mL) butter

❶ In frying pan, heat oil over medium heat. Add onion and sauté for 2 to 3 minutes or until onion is translucent. Add minced garlic.

❷ In cup, mix tomato paste and water. Add to frying pan with tomato, sugar, basil, oregano, salt and pepper, and simmer gently for 10 minutes. Add clams and juice and simmer for another 2 to 3 minutes.

❸ In large pot, bring salted water to boil. Add pasta and stir until water returns to boil. Cook uncovered, stirring occasionally, for 6 to 7 minutes or until *al dente* (tender but not soft).

❹ Drain pasta, pile onto warm plate and toss with butter. Ladle clam sauce on top.

SUNLIGHT DOESN'T RIPEN TOMATOES, WARMTH DOES.

FIND A SPOT NEAR THE STOVE WHERE THEY CAN GET

A LITTLE HEAT.

■ ■

Italy

PASTA WITH WALNUTS
(Salsa di Noci)

SERVES ONE

Nut sauce is a good choice in early winter when few fresh vegetables are at bargain prices. Late apples are ripe, and diced with celery and dressed with lemon juice, make a refreshing contrast to creamy pasta.

1 tbsp (15 mL) butter
½ cup (125 mL) walnuts, roughly chopped
4 tbsp (60 mL) heavy cream
2 tbsp (25 mL) grated Parmesan cheese
Salt and pepper to taste
⅓ lb (150 g) dried fettuccine or spaghetti

❶ In frying pan, melt butter over medium-low heat. Add walnuts, cream, Parmesan cheese, salt and pepper. Cook gently for 3 to 4 minutes.

❷ In large pot, bring water to boil. Add salt, if desired. Add fettuccine and stir until water returns to boil. Cook uncovered, stirring occasionally, for 6 to 8 minutes or until *al dente* (tender but not soft).

❸ Drain and immediately toss with walnut mixture. Pile onto warm plate.

To freshen stale nuts, place in an uncovered pan and bake at 250° F (120° C) for 6 to 8 minutes.

■■■■■■■■■■■■■■■■■■■■■■■■■■■■■■■■

Italy

BACON, EGGS 'N CHEESE PASTA

(Spaghetti alla Carbonara)

This delicious spaghetti from Rome is one of the fastest meals I know. I always serve it with green peas but any favorite green vegetable would be a colorful accompaniment.

4 to 6 oz (125 to 170 g) dried spaghetti
2 tbsp (25 mL) olive or canola oil
2 or 3 strips of bacon, cut into bits
3 tbsp (45 mL) grated Parmesan cheese
2 eggs, beaten with a fork
Black pepper to taste

SERVES ONE

❶ In large pot, bring water to boil. Add salt, if desired. Add pasta and stir until water returns to boil. Cook uncovered, stirring occasionally, for 6 to 8 minutes or until *al dente* (tender but not soft).

❷ Meanwhile, heat oil in frying pan and cook bacon until crisp.

❸ Drain spaghetti, saving 4 tbsp (60 mL) of the cooking water. Return spaghetti and cooking water to pot. Pour in olive oil. Add cooked bacon bits, Parmesan cheese, beaten eggs and pepper, and quickly toss. (The heat of the pasta will cook the eggs.)

❹ Pile onto warm plate, sprinkle with extra Parmesan cheese, if desired, and dig in!

READY GRATED PARMESAN CHEESE IS OFTEN CHEAPER THAN A WEDGE OF IMPORTED ITALIAN PARMESAN, BUT IT MAY CONTAIN FILLERS. FOR THE BEST FLAVOR, GRATE YOUR OWN AND STORE IN THE FREEZER.

■ ■

Canada

MACARONI AND CHEESE
(Le Macaroni au sauce de fromage)

Macaroni and cheese has been a favorite budget supper in North America since 1937 when Kraft Dinner or "KD" first hit the market. There are innumerable "from scratch" versions, but this one with Cheddar cheese sauce adapts well to a single serving and can be doubled with success. Serve with sliced tomato sprinkled with basil, a few chopped nuts and a squeeze of lemon.

1½ cups (375 mL) macaroni or rotini
2 or 3 slices cooked bacon (optional)

··

Cʜᴇᴇsᴇ Sᴀᴜᴄᴇ
2 tbsp (25 mL) butter or canola oil
2 tbsp (25 mL) all-purpose flour
¾ cup (175 mL) milk
¾ cup (175 mL) grated Canadian cheddar cheese
Salt and pepper to taste
Pinch dry mustard (optional)

❶ *Cheese Sauce:* In heavy-bottomed saucepan, melt butter over medium heat and add flour. Whisk vigorously for 1 minute. Slowly stir in milk and whisk until thickened and smooth. Reduce heat to low and add cheese and seasonings. Stir until cheese is melted. Do not boil after adding cheese. For a thinner sauce, add more milk.

❷ Meanwhile, bring large pot of salted water to boil. Add macaroni and stir until water returns to boil. Cook uncovered, stirring occasionally, for 8 to 10 minutes or until *al dente* (tender but not soft). Drain and mix with cheese sauce.

❸ Spoon into warm bowl and top with bacon, if using.

CHEDDAR CHEESE SAUCE IS ALSO DELICIOUS WITH BAKED POTATOES AND GREEN VEGETABLES, ON CRUNCHY NACHOS WITH SALSA, AND OVER OMELETS OR POACHED EGGS.

■■■■■■■■■■■■■■■■■■■■■■■■■■■■■■

Morocco, Algeria and Tunisia

COUSCOUS

This tiny, grain-like pellet of semolina wheat dough origi-nated in North Africa. True couscous takes time to prepare but now an instant or precooked one is available that takes just minutes to cook. Serve with Sweet and Spicy Meatballs (page 120) or simmered vegetables.

¾ (175 mL) cup water
½ tsp (2 mL) salt (optional)
½ cup (125 mL) instant couscous
1 tbsp (15 mL) butter

❶ In saucepan, bring water to boil. Add salt, if desired. Add couscous and butter and stir well. Cover pan, remove from heat and let stand and steam for 5 minutes. Uncover and fluff with a fork.

QUICK VEGETABLE TAGINE

1 cup (250 mL) tomato juice
2 cups (500 mL) diced favorite vegetables
¼ cup (50 mL) cooked chick-peas
3 tbsp (45 mL) raisins
½ tsp (2 mL) salt
¼ tsp (1 mL) each cinnamon and ground cloves
Pinch cayenne pepper

❶ In covered saucepan, simmer all ingredients over medium heat for 15 minutes or until tender. Ladle over couscous.

BASIC KITCHEN EQUIPMENT

With kitchen equipment, less is often better than more. Try to avoid accepting everyone's castoffs; thin, wobbly, aluminum saucepans with no lids, stainless steel knives that are dull, and light-weight frying pans that have lost their non-stick coating. Not only will most budget cooks not have the storage space, but the results of cooking with these gifts, will be disappointing. Don't overlook the possibility of finding excellent pots, pans and utensils at garage sales, junk shops and school and church fairs. Some items that will have cost next to nothing will last a lifetime.

Knives and Chopping Board

You will need at least three knives: ❶ A basic carbon steel French chef's knife. Stainless steel cannot be sharpened. Use a carborundum or sharpening steel to keep a good edge and never put it in a dishwasher; ❷ A saw-edged bread knife (also good for slicing tomatoes); ❸ A small, hooked paring knife for deboning chicken, and peeling fruit and vegetables.

Spoons and Tongs

One or two long handled wooden spoons for stirring and a slotted (with holes) metal spoon for stir-frying is adequate. Tongs are useful when grilling and frying to turn food without piercing.

Vegetable Peeler

A small and inexpensive swivel-bladed peeler is perfect for peeling potatoes, and thin slices of orange or lemon peel.

Can Opener

An all-in-one, can opener, bottle opener and cork screw is ideal.

Grater or Shredder

This inexpensive 4 slice grater is invaluable. Use it to shred vegetables for salad or potato pancakes, shred cheese for pizza, and grate lemon or orange peel (zest).

Sieve or Colander

Find a large, metal (plastic will melt) sieve for rinsing rice, draining pasta and vegetables, washing lettuce and spinach. A colander is fine too but make sure the holes are not too big or rice will fall through.

Spatula and Whisk

A spatula or flipper is useful for lifting eggs and fish, turning pancakes and fried rice. A whisk is essential for lump-free sauces and gravies, beating eggs and whipping cream.

Frying Pans

Small and medium sized, heavy-bottomed frying pans with oven-proof handles and lids. I prefer cast iron pans with iron or heavy glass lids. They will not rust if scrubbed with salt rather than abrasive cleansers and lightly wiped with oil before storing. Non-stick pans can scratch and lose their coating if burnt.

Wok

You can stir-fry with a frying pan, but a wok is a wonderful light weight pan for cooking over high heat. It is easy to move with one hand on and off the heat source for temperature control. For use with an electric stove, choose a wok with a slightly flattened bottom, or hot spot.

Corked Bottle

Cut a deep wedge shape from one side of a cork and use it to stopper a wine bottle filled with cooking oil (canola) or vinegar. This regulates the flow and prevents the contents from gushing out when only a drop or two is needed.

Saucepans

Three saucepans with lids would be ideal; a small one for boiling eggs and heating a cup of soup, a medium one for cooking sauces and vegetables , and a large one for boiling pasta, rice, and making soup stock. The medium pot should have a flat heavy bottom if possible. It heats evenly and is less likely to scorch. Choose pots with oven-proof handles.

Broiler Pan and Rack

Most older stoves will have lost their broiler pans. For quick broiling and toasting bread, one will be needed. Substitute a shallow roasting pan and a wire rack. The roasting pan can also double as a fish poacher.

Pie Plate and Pizza Pan

For a single person a small 6″ (15cm) pie plate is a useful size to use as a casserole or oven-to-table plate. A medium round pizza pan, can easily double as a small cookie sheet, an open-face sandwich or bruchetta grill, a cake platter and a lid for a large pot or pan.

Mixing Bowls

Try to find bowls that stack inside one another, if storage is a problem. A coffee mug is fine for a small mixing bowl. Junk or second-hand stores often carry beautiful bone china bowls that have lost their lids and they make perfect mixing and serving bowls.

Measuring Cups and Spoons

Personally, I seldom measure but rely on taste and appetite to determine amounts. Start with too little, you can always add more but you cannot take away, if a dish is too salty, overly sweet or burning hot.

Miscellaneous

There are a lot of fabulous cooks who have never owned and would not thank you for designer gadgets and processors. However the following list may make your meal preparation easier; a collapsible steaming rack for the inside of a saucepan, scissors (cutting herbs), secateurs (cutting chicken) needle-nose pliers (deboning fish), bamboo steamer (reheating leftovers), mortar and pestle (for crushing herbs and spices), Chinese cleaver (hacking chicken, pounding fillets flat, crushing garlic), meat skewers, and a kitchen fire extinguisher.

USEFUL HERB AND SPICE MIXTURES

Even the plainest and most humble of foods can be given an inexpensive lift with the addition of herbs and spices. To save money, avoid brand names with fancy bottles and packages. Dried herbs can lose pungency so buy in small quantities and store in your own airtight jars. To bring out the full natural oils and aroma of dried herbs, crush between the palms of your hands before adding to dishes. Spices and seeds can be bought ready and ground or they can be crushed in a mortar and pestle or in a small wooden bowl with a wooden spoon. The following international spice mixtures are meant to be a guide only, and you are encouraged to experiment with your own combinations and personalize your *Frugal Feasts*.

Caribbean Mix (jerk spice)
Marinate chicken, pork or tofu in this fiery combination of spices moistened with fruit juice before grilling in the oven or barbecue.Combine and crush an equal amount of allspice, cinnamon, nutmeg, thyme and sugar with black pepper and cayenne to taste.

Chinese 5 Powder Spice (heung new fun)
Two of the five powders are difficult to find but do not let that deter you from trying this classic spice mixture using only the first three. Use in chicken and pork dishes or mix sparingly into ground meat burgers. The five powders include: cloves, cinnamon and fennel (a slightly licorice aroma), ground licorice root and star anise.

French Herb Mix (herbes de Provence)

This is one of my favorite mixes for scrambled eggs, salads and soups (especially tomato soup). Combine and crush two parts marjoram, thyme and savory to one part dried rosemary, sage, mint and lavender flowers.

Greek Mix (rigani ke arismari)

I cannot imagine grilling lamb chops or sausage with out a sprinkle of this aromatic combination of equal parts oregano and rosemary.

Indian Curry (masala)

There are many varieties of commercial curry powders on the market that are very good but it is fun to mix your own. This is a mild one that I favor although it is not nearly hot enough for my brother-in-law who was born in Bihar, India. Combine and crush three parts tumeric, coriander seeds and cumin seeds to one part ground cinnamon, cloves, nutmeg, ginger and cardamom seeds. Add black pepper and cayenne to taste.

Iranian Spice Mix (advieh)

I will never forget the first time I tasted the incredibly delicious and spicy ground lamb patties *luleh kabab* on the streets of Teheran. As well as patties, sprinkle on meats for barbecue, and mix into rice. Combine and crush two parts ground cinnamon to one part cardamom seeds, tumeric, nutmeg, cumin and coriander. Use sparingly, as it is very aromatic.

Italian Mix (un po' di aromi)

This combination of herbs is essential to meat and tomato sauces, perks up salads and omelets, and improves commercial mass produced pizza. Combine and crush equal parts of basil, oregano and sweet marjoram.

Mexican Chili Mix
This mixture can be as fiery hot or as gentle as you wish. Combine and crush equal parts of oregano and cumin with hot dried chile pepper to taste.

Seafood Seasoning
Equal parts of crushed tarragon and dill complement most fish dishes, whether a tuna fish sandwich, a cold seafood salad or an herb butter to melt over hot grilled fish. Dill and tarragon are also excellent with mushrooms and sprinkled on roast chicken.

Salad Seasoning (fine herbs)
If you have just the tiniest patch of garden, or a balcony planter box, consider growing mint, chives and parsley. They are hardy plants and a great addition to fresh vegetable salads.

INDEX
(*denotes vegetarian dish)

St. Lucia
le potage au potiron
(pumpkin soup)* 30
Sweden
små köttbullar (meatballs
in cream) 119
Switzerland
croque-monsieur (toasted
ham and cheese) 20

T
Thailand
mah mee (spicy noodles)
123
Turkey
iç pilav (spicy golden
rice)* 70
fasulye pilaki (byzantine
beans)* 77
şehriyeli çorbasi (chicken
soup) 32

U
United States
Boston clam chowder 29
California lemon chicken
104
parmesan potato wedges*
50
polenta with walnuts,
garlic and pears 134
spinach fettuccine with
vegetables and ham
143
southern fried chicken
100

V
Vegetarian dishes marked
with*

W, X, Y, Z